THE ELSEWHEREANS

ALSO BY JEET THAYIL

FICTION

Names of the Women

Low

The Book of Chocolate Saints

Narcopolis

POETRY

The City under the City (with John Kinsella)

I'll Have It Here

Collected Poems

These Errors Are Correct

English

Apocalypso

Gemini (Two-Poet Volume with Vijay Nambisan)

AS EDITOR

The Penguin Book of Indian Poets

The Bloodaxe Book of Contemporary Indian Poets

Divided Time: India and the End of Diaspora

LIBRETTI

Babur in London

Extinction Violin

Praise for

THE ELSEWHEREANS

'*The Elsewhereans* is a wonderfully rich evocation of the era of decolonization and non-alignment, and the peripatetic lives and multiple perspectives that it made possible. Reading it, I felt like I was meeting many ghosts from my own past.'

AMITAV GHOSH

'Like the "river of three rivers" at its heart, *The Elsewhereans* surges forward in multiple narrative currents: autofiction, Künstlerroman, mourning diary. Dispensing with conventional notions of plot, Thayil draws on real and imagined archives, testimonies and anecdotes to trace the wanderings of a family from Kerala to places as disparate as Bombay, Hanoi, Paris, Elmau and Algeciras. But it is above all his sentences – mercurial, witty, luminous – that pull us through each new and unexpected encounter. The result is a hauntingly lyrical meditation on migration, belonging and grief. *The Elsewhereans* is Thayil at his finest yet.'

DEVIKA REGE

'How can a book so melancholy also be so exhilarating? *The Elsewhereans* blurs timezones and timelines as it traces the wanderings of a family across rivers and oceans, across silences and stories. It is equally attentive to the politics of nation-building and family caretaking. The centre of this dazzling spiral novel is deep love, examined with ruthless poetic precision, and found to be flawed but essential for survival.'

SHAHNAZ HABIB

'Jeet Thayil just keeps getting better and better: this is writing of great skill and precision, charm and warmth, beauty and wit, taut as a coiled spring, laced with pin-sharp, pitch-perfect dialogue. *The Elsewhereans* could well be Thayil's masterpiece.'

WILLIAM DALRYMPLE

THE ELSEWHEREANS

A Documentary Novel

Jeet Thayil

FOURTH ESTATE · *New Delhi*

First published in India by Fourth Estate 2025
An imprint of HarperCollins *Publishers*
HarperCollins *Publishers* India, Cyber City, Building 10-A, Gurugram, Haryana – 122002, India
www.harpercollins.co.in

2 4 6 8 10 9 7 5 3 1

P-ISBN: 978-93-6989-779-7
E-ISBN: 978-93-6989-986-9

Book design by Bonita Vaz-Shimray

Printed and bound at
Thomson Press (India) Ltd

*

HarperCollins Publishers, Macken House, 39/40 Mayor Street Upper, Dublin 1,
D01 C9W8, Ireland

MIX
Paper | Supporting responsible forestry
FSC® C010615

This book is produced from independently certified FSC® paper
to ensure responsible forest management.

To my mother, Ammu George (1934–2025),
who preferred the fictional over the real

'When a writer is born into a family,
the family is finished.'
CZESŁAW MIŁOSZ

'O Fathers, do not provoke your children,
lest they become discouraged.'
Colossians 3:21

'You are woman, you are man; you are boy, you are girl;
as an old man you totter along on your cane;
you are born with your face turned everywhere.'
***Shvetashvatara Upanishad* 4:3**

'Modern scholarship suggests that the hermaphroditic nature of plants – as they possess both penis and vagina in the same physical organism – recalls the androgynous ancestors from which all human life descended.'
CHACHIAMMA JACOB,
The Classification of Angels: A Traveller's Handbook

'You got to tell me, brave Captain,
Why are the wicked so strong?
How do the angels get to sleep
When the Devil leaves the porch light on?'
TOM WAITS, *'Mr Siegel'*

'The past only comes back when the present runs so smoothly that it is like the sliding surface of a deep river. Then one sees through the surface to the depths. In those moments I find one of my greatest satisfactions, not that I am thinking of the past; but that it is then that I am living most fully in the present. For the present when backed by the past is a thousand times deeper than the present when it presses so close that you can feel nothing else...'
VIRGINIA WOOLF, ***Moments of Being***

'And where would you like to be, after all?'
'Anywhere but here.'
A.T. MARKOSE, ***epigraph to 'Inside Baudelaire'***

'I never grew up, it's getting so old.'
TAYLOR SWIFT, ***'The Archer'***

'Old age is a shipwreck.'
AMMU GEORGE

'Yet why not say what happened?'
ROBERT LOWELL, ***'Epilogue'***

The real names and photographs in these pages are fictions.
The fictional names and events are documentary.
The truth, as we know, lies in between.

CONTENTS

HOTEL
JANPATH
NEW DELHI
INDIA

THE HOUSE ON RIVER-OF-THREE-RIVERS

MAMALASSERY, 1957 | BOMBAY, 1957 | MAMALASSERY, 1959 | BOMBAY, 1964

If memory could speak, what would it say? Only lies. Beautiful lies quietly said with a straight face and a pure heart. And in the saying, the lies, of every colour and size and degree of intent, all the lies would be true. As here, at the start, where memory might say something as plain and clear as this: All stories begin with a river, and end with one. And you might say in reply, Yes, I believe this to be true.

UNCHAPERONED, HE MEETS HER. It leads to gossip on both sides. He's seen a photograph, the families have met, what more is needed? A word: yes or no. Instead, he makes a note of the address, books a flight to Cochin, and rents a car that takes him to the high school in Alwaye.

He asks for Ammu Thomas.

The mathematics teacher runs into the staffroom and says there's a man at the gate asking for her. To mask her excitement, the teacher is unnaturally calm.

'What?' says Ammu. 'Speak up, girl.'

'He has a beard,' says the mathematics teacher. 'Full!'

'Who does?'

'One man has come to see you.'

Ammu rushes out sure that something has happened, an emergency. Her father has hurt himself. Or her mother. An accident…

The bearded man introduces himself as a journalist from Bombay and produces a photograph from his wallet. She peers: it takes a moment to recognize the girl in the picture. Taken in her last year at school, hair in disarray, indelibly silly smile on her face. Not her favourite photo by a long shot. But she is posing with the trophies she won as a school athletics champion. She understands now who he is and why he's come to see her. Minutely she examines his eyes hidden behind sunglasses.

'Twenty-seven medals and twenty-five cups,' Ammu says.

'For running and swimming and all those good things,' he says.

'Correct!'

'You *sound* like a teacher. What subject do you teach?'

'Physics, chemistry, biology.'

'Very good. In my opinion…'

'But what does opinion have to do with it?'

He takes off his sunglasses: the eyes are grey.

'In my opinion, the photo does you no justice at all.'

He's looking not just at Ammu but at the entirety of the picture she makes. The simple cotton sari with a red border, the string of jasmines in her flyaway hair, the shy smile and clever eyes. Her beauty. He offers the boiled sweets he slipped into his pocket on the Air India flight and she accepts, charmed, seeing it for what it is, a gesture by a man with a peculiar sense of romance and a grand idea of himself.

'Gratitude, great gratitude,' she says formally. Already the sweets are sticky in her hand. 'I have to go now.'

The meeting is over and the message goes to both families.

George returns to Bombay and flies to Harrisburg, Pennsylvania, where he will teach journalism for three months. For his first international flight, he wears a bow tie and suit, on his arm a heavy overcoat for cold American weather. The TWA Super Constellation stops at Cairo, Rome and Washington, DC. He arrives at JFK after a day of travel, new suit crumpled, the overcoat conspicuous, embarrassing, an inexperienced traveller's mistake. It is the beginning of summer. He's misjudged the weather.

'Kochay,' he writes to Ammu, addressing her with the Malayalam for *child*, as he will even when she is an old woman. 'Everything is different here but also the same. The days are sunny and hot, not as hot as Bombay but almost! Their houses are full of gadgets and no servants. Even poor people drive cars ... I think I like the American face. They go out of their way to appear cheerful at all times, especially when they're sad. This is the main difference between Americans and Indians. We try always to appear gloomy, especially when we are happy. Once you get used to the difference, you fit right in.'

She replies by return mail.

'Learn everything you can about the American face. One day we may go there. We may go anywhere. I am a great believer in foreign travel! I read your letter often and then home feels foreign. The summer holidays have started. I'm in Mamalassery. I miss teaching and I miss Alwaye, but not much. When are you coming back?'

The date is fixed for two weeks after his return in August.

A WEEK BEFORE THE WEDDING, a dozen tents appear between the house and the steps that lead to the river.

Thommen is summoned, a wedding cook famous for his bad temper and his red meen curry. He arrives with an assistant and a cartload of clay pots, knives, cauldrons, an assortment of long metal ladles and short ones made of coconut shells, bunches of fresh and dried herbs, bundles of rich chammandi powder made with a well-guarded list of ingredients committed to memory, and a barrel of his own coconut oil. His assistant, a woman with a temper as unpredictable as Thommen's, takes a tent as her own. He calls her his wife although his wife is long gone, unable to reconcile to the gypsy lifestyle and the violence she was forced to endure for most of her marriage. His road-wives change at will, and they share a quality with his curries. Extreme volatility. During the season, Thommen travels for months at a time. Depending on the size of the wedding and the payment, he stays for a few days or a week.

His meen curry is a purist's invention that uses only seven ingredients: hand-picked chunks of kingfish, fistfuls of red chilli powder, rock salt, mustard seeds, a hint of diced shallots, ginger, and the precious coal-black lumps of Malabar tamarind he sources from Alleppey and secretes among his personal effects. He refuses to sully the dish with those ingredients he deems contaminants: curry leaves, green chillies, coconut milk and fenugreek. The result is fiery, glazed with a thick layer of coconut oil, and tastes best a day after cooking, so Thommen makes vast quantities in advance, filling clay pot after clay pot. Everything else he'll make on the morning of the wedding. Pork ghee roast. Egg roast. Beef fry with coconut. Mountains of white rice and hillocks of red. Papadums with no gleam of the oil in which they've been deep-fried, only the aroma. Appams fermented with a touch of sweet-and-sour toddy. Tapioca steamed plain and unsalted, purposely bland to complement the tear-inducing fish curry. Pan-fried shrimps. Fried sardines marinated in red chilli, turmeric and salt. Chicken stew creamy with coconut milk, diced potatoes and carrots. Thin seer-fish cutlets. These are traditional preparations served at every wedding. But Thommen excels in items no other wedding cook would attempt. Rabbit stewed for three hours with chunks of raw jaggery and home-made wine. Batter-fried frog's legs with tamarind–pineapple pachadi. Deep-fried anchovies for 'touchings.' Raw mango and sweet lime pickle for 'lickings.' Dosas stuffed with sweet crabmeat. Stingray steaks served with ginger chutney and cut carrot pickle, with a lethal coconut–prawn gunpowder podi on the side.

While cooking, Thommen drinks. Fresh toddy in the morning and fermented toddy in the afternoon. After sunset, he switches to arrack. The lamp in his tent burns half the night. At two or three in the morning come the screams of his current wife. High-pitched. Ungrammatical. Unhinged. 'Which woman stay with you?' Thommen does not reply, and his silence infuriates her more than any words he might fling. 'Old man. No teeth. What good?' It's true that some of Thommen's teeth are missing. His food is slow-cooked over wood fires and known as melt-in-the-mouth for this reason. It's the only way he can enjoy his own food. The reference to his teeth gives her the response she's been craving. He beats her. She beats him. There follow the sounds of violent lovemaking. The smack, the moan, the rhythmic bed-creak. Next morning, it's business as usual. At night, the scenario repeats.

The house has seen countless couplings, weddings, births, deaths.

On the exact spot where Anniethottam now stands, the king of Travancore once built a pleasure station, a stop during his boating trips to replenish the jaded royal spirits with toddy, tapioca and fried fish. It was well known among the populace that the king's tastes in food were identical to any peasant's, a quality that made him beloved among the people. According to Thomas family legend, the land was a royal gift to an ancestor who'd gone above and beyond his duty as a citizen when the king stopped at Mamalassery during the hot season. This early Thomas served a prize pig roasted with sweet bananas, Kolumbu mangoes and duck's eggs, and tapped enough toddy to keep the king's entourage watered until late evening. The king showed his appreciation by presenting him with the stretch of riverfront on which the pleasure station stood. The land came with the toddy-tappers and peasants who lived on it, whose descendants would also toil for the house.

The Thomas ancestor who established the family's fortunes is buried at Mamalassery church along with his sons and daughters. Grandsons and granddaughters, squeezed out due to lack of space at the cemetery, are buried around the general vicinity of the church. Sometimes during the rainy season when there is a landslide, their bones are found mixed with mud and unimaginable litter and dog faeces. The passing villager who comes across these bones nudges them into the ditch by the side of the road or kicks them forcefully into the river.

In the early twentieth century, the current Thomas rebuilds the house as close as possible to the Muvattupuzha, river-of-three-rivers. His intention is to bathe in the river every morning of his life. The old house once had another name, long gone, remembered by nobody. He names the new one after a daughter who dies of brain fever, and the house and land come to be called Anniethottam: Annie's Place.

As the days pass, wedding guests start to arrive. Because it is in a remote spot inaccessible by road, older guests are brought on the river in a hired boat. Three days before Ammu's wedding, a grand-uncle, Bobben, misses the express train from Trichur. Phone calls are made and new plans hatched. He takes the last boat, meant to leave before sunset, but there is an unexplained delay. From George's side of the family, landlubbers all, Grand-Uncle Bobben has never learned how to swim. The full current and the pitch darkness of night on the river make him nervous. The wedding presents he has packed, a silk sari for the bride and a gold-bordered lungi for the groom, are soaked by the river water gathered in the hold. The boat hits a number of big swells near Maneed and the boatmen struggle to navigate the current. The guests are told to hold on to their seats. Bobben's is slippery, and his soft hands cannot find purchase. To calm himself, he repeats the quadratic equation he teaches to his class of distracted boys, some of whom must be persuaded with a ruler across the palm depending on the severity of the offence. 'Four x squared minus five x minus twelve equals zero,' he repeats, his eyes closed. The river kicks and the boat bounces and there is an answering kick in his chest. A small animal struggles to escape its tight cage, a violent small animal that wants to kill him. He understands why they call it a heart attack. He *is* under attack. Taken to hospital in the same boat (after it has dropped off the other guests) his condition (touch and go) is kept secret as festivities begin.

Then, two days before the wedding, a new obstacle.

'I'm Hindu more than Christian,' George declares upon arriving at Anniethottam. 'I prefer to not have the ceremony in a church.'

Chachiamma's voice rises over the din.

'Not have the ceremony?'

'In a church.'

'Great God's father! Then where?'

'At a temple or here in the house, anywhere really,' George says mildly, getting up from the oilcloth-covered table in the dining room.

'Hindu,' says Chachiamma. 'I never heard of a Christian Hindu.'

'You must have heard.'

'Never.'

'We were all Hindu once.'

'That was two thousand years ago! Things change. Tell me one thing.'

'But of course,' says George.

'Why did you take so long to give us this important information? Why did you never mention it to my poor daughter?'

'Nobody asked.'

'Clean-shave,' says Jacob, Ammu's youngest brother who will become the master, modernizer and scourge of Anniethottam. 'Complete clean-shave,' he says, his voice full of admiration.

Ammu's sisters have come from Trichur and Trivandrum for the wedding, and now it appears there won't be one. They rush to tell her about her betrothed's secret conversion to Hinduism. She is in the kalapera, the rice harvest storeroom turned into a guest house. Where she will stay until the wedding to prevent any further unscheduled meetings between bride and groom. One of her sisters has already raised an objection based solely on George's beard. Other than the priests, she has never seen a man with a beard. Naturally, she is suspicious. What if it's a way of hiding a disfigurement? What if it covers a cleft lip or birthmark or scar? This is her first objection, an aesthetic one, as she dislikes beards and moustaches, chest hair and neck hair, wrist hair and back hair. Her second objection is more reasonable. If he's Hindu, the marriage is inter-religious. Probably there's a law against it. Or at least a statute. Markose must offer his professional opinion as a lawyer. He'll know if something can be done at this late stage.

But Markose is the only one unfazed by the new development. He's driven from Cochin to Mamalassery in his famous Morris Oxford, stopping at the toll booths, not stopping at the toddy shops, taking a break only for a glass of roadside tea. He parks the prized automobile safely at his brother Chellan's house on the main road, and walks across the paddies and narrow mud culverts to Anniethottam. The trip has taken two and a half hours from door to door, and he's in no mood for delay.

He takes George aside.

'Summit meeting,' he says. 'Come with me.'

He leads the way, past the front room where the family can be heard lamenting their choice of son-in-law, past the back porch where Ammu's brothers are smoking beedis and drinking rum out of chai glasses (one is in the army and he gets crates of rum at a heavily discounted price), past the grinding room where even at this hour Thommen is noisily hammering a man-sized mortar into a giant pestle to make more of his secret chammandi, past the neem, jackfruit and lemon trees, and into the yard fronting the river. Markose has come directly from the office. He wears a dark suit and tie, and the humidity is too much for him.

'I should have worn a lungi,' he says, sweating freely, his regret plain to see. George likes the man.

'Brother, listen,' says Markose, taking off his jacket. His white shirt has soaked through in patches. 'I believe I have a solution to our current imbroglio.'

'I'm glad somebody does,' says George, taking a seat on the stone bench that faces the river. He hears it flowing ahead of him, vast and oblivious, into the new unknown world.

'But first, is it true you went to see Ammu without telling anyone?'

'It is.'

'Well, let's hear it. Don't leave out a thing.'

George tells him about the flight to Cochin, the rented car, the meeting at the gate, the photograph, the fact that he had to see her before agreeing to marriage and that she had to see him.

'My dear fellow,' says Markose, 'all I can say is, well done. One admires the pluck! Now look here, the church has been reserved and the priests paid. Invitations have gone out. A hundred and fifty guests are on their way. In short, your religious conversion is somewhat untenable.' Markose is pacing in front of the bench as though he were at the Supreme Court. 'Moreover, I am of the same opinion as you. People should leave the church and go back to God, as the French philosopher said. Nevertheless...'

'Correction. I think people should leave the church and go back to the temple,' says George. 'That's what I really think.'

He's delighted to see that his mention of temples has robbed Markose of speech, though no doubt only temporarily. His future brother-in-law is a lawyer and international jurist, famous for his peppery rhetoric. It is rare to find him at a loss for words.

Markose stops his pacing and sits heavily on the bench. His belly strains against his belt. The Old Spice he favours, for the sailing ship on its white buoy-shaped bottle, drips in rivulets from his cheeks. His neatly parted hair has lost its authority.

'Yes, yes, yes,' says Markose. 'In any case, here's my solution.'

'I am happy to hear it.'

'Let's try a plea bargain. If you agree to the church ceremony, I will insist that no one pressures you to attend Sunday services in the future.'

'Ever?'

'Ever is a problematic concept, but let us agree. *Ever*.'

There's a brief pause while George considers the merits of the bargain. He becomes aware of the sounds of the evening. High rattle of crickets. River noise on the wind. The unseen bird Ammu calls the beauty bird because its cry is *pretty, pretty, pretty*. To his ears it sounds more like *pity, pity, pity*. Somewhere in the distance, a big dog barks at regular intervals. Every other minute, *bark, bark, bark*. George examines the trees. Lemon, mango, possibly jackfruit: and this is as far as it goes, his knowledge of the flora in these parts. There are dozens of trees and flowering plants he's never seen in his life. Anniethottam is a jungle, bewilderingly tropical.

'And one more thing,' says Markose.

'I thought there might be.'

'Please stop saying you're Hindu. In my opinion, one's religious inclinations, like one's sexual habits, should remain private.'

'Well, when you put it that way,' says George, who is nothing if not amenable to a reasonable request. 'May I ask you a question?'

Markose pulls loose his tie and unbuttons his collar.

'When a Kerala Christian bride comes into her marriage home, she crosses the threshold with her right foot, isn't that correct?'

Markose produces a handkerchief and mops his face. He wipes his neck and his hands, and starts again on his face.

'But that is a Hindu custom and a marker of caste.'

Markose sits on the bench and hastily rolls up his sleeves.

'You have to choose, don't you see? You can't call yourself a Christian yet keep the markers of your high Hindu caste. Bad manners. Reeks of hypocrisy if not systemic class manipulation.'

Markose looks up at the sky as though he's asking God for help. He uses the handkerchief and wishes for a river bath. He wonders if the young journalist is a communist, which would make him a Hindu Christian communist. What next? He says, 'I'll put it to them, but I think it is a fait accompli. Ammu shall be allowed to enter her marital home with whichever foot she damn well chooses.'

He rises and holds out his hand. They shake on the deal with the silent regard of the soon-to-be-kin.

But in the house the drama plays on, and as always Ammu's father Thomas is nowhere to be seen. If someone had walked to the front gate, they would have seen his tall, bony silhouette at the edge of the rice fields, holding a staff as tall as he, hooked nose pointing in the direction of the setting sun. He prefers the company of the river and the scratchy laughter of the cormorant to four walls and the pitch of human voices.

Ammu's sisters are waiting in the dining room. One gives George a shred of lined paper with some English words written in pencil, 'PLEASE DON'T BE STUBBORN', in Ammu's clear schoolteacher's script.

THE CEREMONY TAKES PLACE at Mamalassery church.

The feast begins at noon. Three hundred appams are served with egg roast, papadums, and goat stewed in coconut milk. Several dozen cases of rum are opened and emptied. Three hundred and thirty cups of tea are served, with banana fritters and without. Of the one hundred and ninety-nine guests, one hundred and eighty are relatives and associates of the Thomas line, distant, close and neither-close-nor-distant. The remaining eighteen are George's family and a colleague, Raghavan, loyal member of the Communist Party of India, conflicted communist embarrassed that he has a full-time job with a popular Bombay tabloid. His sympathies are with the low-caste servers who pick up after the wedding guests, but his place on the table is among their class enemies. He drains his glass of rum, the liquor favoured by the true revolutionaries of Cuba and India. When his glass is empty, he refills and drains it. The collective in which he has found himself, the seething raucous wedding company, has assembled in all its filthy bourgeois decadence, in gold-brocade saris and heavy jewellery, the men sporting orthodox twenty-four carat crosses nestled in tufts of chest hair. Their eyes are glazed and inward-looking. They see only the fish curry and pork roast and chicken biryani, which they attack as if on a battlefield, preceded by their large bellies. Wet rice coats their hands to their wrists, and these they lick clean amid vivid belches and grunts.

A figure totters into the doorway of the eating hall, the light behind him, face in shadow. His arms are spread wide, as if he were Christ on the cross. For a moment the feasters stop their riotous eating, and when he steps into the room they greet him with dismay and surprise. Grand-Uncle Bobben has arrived in his hospital clothes, for he will not miss the wedding meal. He approaches the left side of the hall where George's family is seated – non-swimmers to a man, woman and child: regarded with pity and suspicion by the river-dwellers around them – and the instant he takes his cross-legged place on the floor, a washed banana leaf appears and is filled with a dozen fried, steaming, oozing promontories around a great island of red rice. A tremor of anxiety descends upon the guests as they watch Grand-Uncle Bobben pour a Travancore peg of Solan No. 1 and bat away concerns about his recent heart attack with the retort that his heart is the size of undivided Hindustan, too large to partition or attack.

'God grant long life,' says Father Thurathikkattel, the priest, thick black beard stained with turmeric and red chilli, as he raises a frothy glass of buttermilk. Here comes the gurgling as he empties the buttermilk too quickly, adding clots of foamy white to the stains around his mouth. His round embroidered cap falls askew when he wipes his lips with the back of his hand and uses his little finger to dislodge a piece of kingfish from his teeth. He grabs an appam from a servant passing with a fresh stack, and tears it into large pieces that he dips into the goat stew and stuffs into his mouth with a moan of pleasure.

As if at a signal, the guests fall upon their food with renewed fervour.

'May God grant peace upon you, O flock of the Lord,' says Father Thurathikkattel, raising a steel glass in which a congregant has poured two large pegs of Solan No. 1 – the rotgut reserved for the most exalted of guests – and though the congregation at the feast includes Hindus and Jews and possibly a Muslim or two, today they eat and drink as one, for it is the God of the New Testament that Father Thurathikkattel has invoked and not the unforgiving God of the older book.

'God grant, God grant,' shout his congregants in admiration, raising to the tiled roof hands coated with rice, curry leaves and red gravy.

'God grant?' says Raghavan. 'Grant what?'

'God grant life and wife,' says a man who spits bits of food as he talks, grabbing a handful of fried beef, some of which he deposits on his leaf and some on the bare feet of the nearest guest.

Entirely by chance, Raghavan has been placed next to a scion of the landed gentry, a young man named Pathrose who for some reason insists on speaking in English, which compounds his hereditary crime in Raghavan's opinion. Pathrose is proud to say he doesn't believe in equality. He knows he is not equal to Messrs Nehru or Einstein, or the Queen of England. Then how can a labourer on his land think they are equals? 'Maybe I'm not better than Kakkathil Kurumban who works in my fields, but I'm different. Then why we should get equal votes? Universal suffrage means universal suffering!'

Pathrose folds his banana leaf and flings it to the side. He signals for a fresh leaf which immediately is filled with appams and fried beef, wherein he searches out chunks of coconut as if he's sifting for gold. He deftly excavates a handful of clams with his thumb, and demonstrates a preternatural ability to talk and eat at the same time. He expands on the correct way of organizing society – by rank – and sings the praises of tradition. 'The few will always rule the many,' he says, 'whether you like it or not.' He rolls some rice into a ball, dips it in mango pickle, fish curry and chammandi before tossing it in his mouth, talking all the while. The more excited he gets, the more he eats. Now he approaches the real subject of his ire: the tradesmen and workers whose only care in the world is to make money.

'Raghavan, if money is all you care about, then you are unfit to govern. You wait and watch, when the moneymen take over, everything will change,' says Pathrose, washing his hands. 'But not for the better.'

He offers Raghavan an imported Benson & Hedges.

Raghavan has been restless during Pathrose's speech. He refuses the offered cigarette and takes out a beedi, the leaf-rolled poor man's smoke, which he lights with pointed ease. He reminds the other man that it has been only twelve years since the end of a world war waged by those who thought they were purer than everyone else.

'Pathrose, Pathrose,' he says, an expression of infinite sorrow on his face. 'This is the first time we're meeting, but I feel I've known you my whole life. I want to ask you a question: where would we be without the impure, the mixed-up, the mongrel common man? Do we, that is, you and I, have the right to say some men don't deserve to vote?'

'That makes two questions, my dear Raghavan.'

'Two rhetorical questions, Mr Pathrose. You see, I already *know* the answer. More's the pity.'

Beedi enthusiasts call them 'no-speaks' because they go out in an instant. Raghavan's must be relit. Between puffs, he raises a toast to Gramsci's illuminated theory of hegemony and takes a long drink of rum. He has recently acquired a copy of the Italian's *Prison Notebooks* at the second-hand bookstalls near Flora Fountain and is eager to put his investment to use. Balefully, he rises and thunders:

'All men are intellectuals. Let the proletariat become the ruling class. Passive revolution is hogwash. Let the purge begin!'

But the purge will have to wait. His beedi has gone out again and he must ask his antagonist for the use of his Zippo, a tool of cultural hegemony if ever there was one. To Pathrose's mind, socialists are akin to thieves. He keeps a firm hand on his monogrammed lighter.

On and on the two men go, in the ebb and flow of the dance they have performed solo many times in different settings, neither hearing the other, neither heard by the other.

Raghavan drinks too much and eats too little and is soon asleep at his seat, his spectacles fallen on the banana leaf loaded with rice and sambar. There he will stay until he returns to this story in time – in sixteen years, to be exact. Pathrose has eaten too much and drunk too much and he'll stay where he is, too stuffed to get up for sixty-four years, when he'll return as a story within a story.

EARLY ON THE DAY AFTER THE WEDDING, she packs her things. Her mother has prepared cooked food in banana-leaf parcels. There are bottles of boiled water, and books and inflatable pillows. Markose is driving back to Cochin and he offers to drop the new couple to the station. When Ammu sees her mother tearfully nodding goodbye, her own ceremonial tears begin. Her father is nowhere to be found. A gift Thomas nurtures and bestows freely: to vanish when emotion threatens. Her tears subside as they reach the outskirts of Mamalassery, and her brother and oblivious new husband discuss the rain-made dangers of Kerala's roads and how long the drive to Cochin will take.

'What kind of a car is it, though?' asks George, eyeing the wood finish and extra legroom with undisguised envy. It has a comfortable cruising speed of about sixty, and Markose drives with the windows down.

'An endorsement, if any were needed, of the British genius for exploration, assessment of terrain, and conquest,' says Markose.

'We're talking about a car.'

'Most decidedly so, good sir.'

'What about innovation?'

'Very good. Add to the list. What we have here is nothing short of a declaration of supremacy. A shot across the bow. Elegance, function and engineering combined into a single war-ready instrument.'

George assesses his new brother-in-law, the freshly laundered white shirt and narrow black tie, the horn rims, the trimmed moustache and narrow, fastidious lips. He is an unlikely figure in the wilds of Kerala. He is, in fact, unlikely almost anywhere.

'Do you miss it,' says George. 'The Raj?'

'Only on Thursdays,' says Markose. 'But here's a corner of a foreign field that is forever England, and so on ... my Morris Oxford. She takes too much petrol, it's true, but I shall drive no other.'

'I've never seen a colour like this on an automobile.'

'Some among my acquaintances call it cat's eye.'

'Inaccurate, I'd say.'

'I prefer sea-green. For the internal rhyme, if nothing else.'

They talk about atheism versus agnosticism, Bertrand Russell's admiration and jealousy of Wittgenstein, Nehru's reading habits, his soft spot for roses and Englishwomen, Gandhi's experiments with truth and celibacy, and his murder by an RSS man who thought the party wasn't radical enough. When they start on nineteenth-century French poetry, which Ammu knows is an obsession of her brother's, she shuts her eyes and clutches the pillows.

'Why are you so sad, sister?' says Markose, looking at her in the rear-view mirror.

'Not sad, impressed,' she says. 'I just noticed how similar it sounds, RSS and SS. I'm wondering, is it deliberate?'

'Right you are,' says her brother. 'I'd say making a hero out of an assassin is a fairly radical position...'

'Not really. Trotsky's assassin received a Hero of the Soviet Union medal. *And* the Order of Lenin.'

'Not to mention twenty years in a Mexican prison.'

'Not to mention.'

He is sixteen years older. He's never before addressed her as if he were speaking to an adult. As a child, she'd thought of him as a parent rather than a sibling. It strikes her now that she is a married woman embarking on a new life. Her girlhood is over.

At the station, Markose finds a porter to carry their bags.

'If you don't mind, I'd rather not come inside,' he says, shaking George's hand. 'Goodbyes are generally irrelevant, frequently inelegant, and rather somewhat unnecessary, wouldn't you say?'

Ammu knows he's imitating an attitude: his father's. But she is surprised at the emotion on her brother's face.

'Wait,' he says in his gruff, decisive way. 'This is for you.'

A red box, palm-sized, a fine layer of dust on its velvet cover.

'Open at your leisure,' says Markose grandly. 'But for now, sister, hurry or you'll miss the train.'

They have a cabin to themselves. It will be their only time of privacy in the early months of marriage. When the porter is sent off and they settle in for the thirty-hour journey, George begins writing up notes for an editorial to be published in *The Free Press Journal* on the day after they arrive in Bombay. Portuguese Indian troops have opened fire over border rights between two small enclaves in Bombay State. George's editorial is headlined 'Independence When?' Ammu peeks over his shoulder at the first line: *British rule has ended, but what about the Portuguese? Are Indians so habituated to life as colonials that we are unwilling to root out its last vestiges?* At seven-thirty, she opens the banana-leaf parcels Chachiamma has packed. George explains that he is not a devotee of train travel. He prefers not to leave his seat unless immobility is out of the question. Ammu understands: he is giving up responsibility. She takes charge and leaves him to write.

A pattern is being established.

After dinner, a man comes in to make their beds. Fresh white sheets and army blankets with the Indian Railways stamp. When he spreads the sheet for the bottom bunk, a red box falls to the floor and she realizes she's forgotten her brother's gift. She opens the box and finds a delicate gold bracelet with a heart-shaped clasp. On the clasp, an engraved date she'll never forget. She puts it on her wrist and admires the shape it makes.

It is her first time out of Kerala, but the trip is less daunting than expected. She watches the countryside slip past. Ten hours into the journey, the landscape changes from rivers and paddies and lush green fields to dry scrub and barrenness. Waterways disappear. Banana and palm trees disappear. Shop signs change erratically, incomprehensibly. They stop at stations with names she struggles to pronounce. The platform vendors don't speak English or Malayalam or Hindi. The only words she understands are *chai-paani* and *biscoot*. She dozes after lunch and wakes to find a child's hand on her wrist, deftly removing the new bracelet. She snatches it back and hisses at the child, who smiles sweetly. Her mother stands to the side, suckling an infant. Mother and daughter wear low veils that ride up to reveal bright, laughing eyes. They wear patchwork blouses over mirrored red skirts, ivory bangles from wrist to armpit. Tubular silver anklets set off their feet. Silver umbrella pendants dangle from their ears. The child waves as the train pulls out of the platform, and Ammu knows that her foreign travels have properly begun. She keeps her hand close to her heart, holding safe the bracelet with the special date that she has come so close to losing.

In Bombay, they live with George's brother Baby and Baby's wife and two children. The newly married couple sleep on the floor of the front room in the small Mahim flat. To Ammu, the city is too big to visualize except as a collection of pictures: night streets lit yellow by sodium lights, the sea like a circus attraction, crowds at the bus depots and train stations, crowds at the tea shops and bakeries and stores that line the causeways; and on the pavements and against the sea walls, bundled up in the heat, the poor. She cannot connect the city's size with the maps she's seen, and she cannot visualize its shape or density. Most of all, she is awed by how well it is organized. The newspaper man who comes at dawn with a copy of the *Free Press* that George worked on the previous night. The raddiwala in the afternoon who buys old newspapers and magazines by weight. The man on a bicycle who stops twice a day with warm bread in a jute bag. The garbage collectors who appear in the morning and the nightsoil collectors who work in the small hours. The way the gas lamps on the street are lit each evening by a municipal worker who returns at first light to extinguish them. The street-washing trucks that trundle into view at dawn and leave the roads sparkling, the only time of day they'll be this way. It is thrilling to be part of such a system.

But there are adjustments to be made. She is unprepared for housework. She knows how to make tea and little else. Baby's wife, Ellie, an experienced Bombay hand, enlists her as helper. They buy vegetables and fruit at street stalls, the produce spread unevenly on the ground. They stand in the shade and drink coconut water out of straws. The coconuts remind her of Mamalassery. Sometimes, if they don't feel like cooking lunch, they opt for a street-side vada pav or vegetable sandwich on white bread with pumpkin chutney. Ellie, showing off for Ammu, talks to the vendors in Marathi even when they speak to her in Hindi. The city stays up late and wakes up late. After lunch people take a siesta, and have tea at four and dinner at ten. Just as she gets used to the life, Baby learns of an apartment for sale in the same neighbourhood, a two-room ground floor off the main Cadell Road, less than ten minutes from Baby's house and priced at fifteen thousand rupees.

It is Ammu's idea to use the money her father has given them – her dowry, though for reasons of delicacy the word is never used. She and Ellie take a look at it one afternoon. It is only slightly bigger than the Mahim apartment. The front door opens into a short, dark corridor. The kitchen and bath are the same size. A living room and bedroom complete the apartment, and a balcony runs the length of both rooms. They open the door and taste sea salt in the air. At the back of the building, Ammu sees a glint of silver. The Arabian Sea, stretching to the horizon.

'We have to take it. Look at the sea!'

'Never mind the sea,' says Ellie, less impressed. 'The train station is a ten-minute walk.'

George doesn't see the apartment until they move in. He goes to work and she runs the house. The pattern established on the train defines their married life. He earns, she invests. He has no interest in money. She is her father's daughter when it comes to business, surprised at how small his salary is and how easy it is to save. The Cadell Road apartment is the first of many she will buy and sell as their fortunes change. He has nothing when they move in, no kitchen equipment or furniture, not even a stove. The only thing he owns is a two-seater Fiat convertible. They go for drives around the city at night and on holidays, from Cadell Road all the way to Colaba, a twenty-minute run with the wind in her eyes and the car racing along Marine Drive, the top down, a scarf to hold her hair in place. The first sense of freedom she has known. But neither of them knows what to do with freedom, and so it passes without being enjoyed or fully understood.

And soon she is pregnant. He's an assistant editor at *The Free Press Journal*, a venerable Bombay newspaper, she a schoolteacher and athlete. Both have earned master's degrees from decent universities. Bombay has good hospitals, but in the anxiety of the first pregnancy husband and wife revert to type. They make a mistake. She goes home to Kerala, to her mother who has presided over a dozen births. George stays in Bombay.

She's subject to the usual rituals. Coconut oil applications followed by a hot bath, the water heated in a fire-blackened cauldron that has been in the outside washroom for as long as she can remember. A goat is slaughtered and made into hundreds of cups of soup. There's stewed river fish in the day and bone broth at night. A kashayam for morning sickness and another to induce restful sleep. She's in the kitchen in the evening, adding honey to the kashayam, when she hears a thud from the yard, a sound she knows from her childhood: a ripe kadukachi has fallen to the ground. It takes her some time to find it, slightly crushed and burst on the side. She tears the skin with her teeth and eats the sticky fist-sized mango as she walks back to the house. For the rest of her stay at Anniethottam, a part of her listens for the sound of her childhood, craving sweetness.

Early one afternoon, the sun turns hazy and the breeze drops. A blanket of moisture hangs in the air. The birds set up a commotion as they fly to their night-time roosts in the middle of the day. In minutes, the sky changes from mauve to grey to black. There's a crack of thunder and veined lightning in the gloom. The river reeks of fish spawn and leaf mould. It seems as if all of Mamalassery is about to sink into the marshland from which it rose. The wet season is about to begin.

Chachiamma shuts the windows, bunches the curtains up on their hooks and sends the washerwoman Kunjukali to collect the clothes drying on lines in the yard. Quickly, the boats are secured and a meal made for the evening. Ammu sits on the porch and watches Kunjukali struggle with the saris, towels and bed sheets flapping in the wind. She waits. It's a kind of happiness to endure darkness in the afternoon with the expectation of rain.

At first, fat drops crash against the tin roof of the boathouse. The dust around the entrance gate rolls into tiny balls of mud and the gravel darkens. The first drops are heavy but infrequent. Then comes rain so continuous, she can hear nothing else. It punches through the leaves of the banana trees in the front yard. The wind picks up, pushing the rain into right angles. The shuttered windows crash against the wall. Very quickly, the front yard is flooded. The deluge doesn't let up for four days. The river overgrows its banks, joins the flooded fields, and makes the house a new island. For a month and more, Anniethottam will be accessible only by canoe. Because of the flooding, the midwife they rely upon has to return to her village to care for her parents. Chachiamma decides to try someone new – and the opiated midwife comes into their lives.

The opium would have been intended for the massive containers of the East India Company. There would have been bills of lading and receipts, handwritten records in triplicate, stages by which the drug was diverted from the ports of Calcutta and Bombay to a village in the south and then into the midwife's cup. She doesn't know any of this, the routes the drug took to get to her, or the close connection between the opium merchants and the distant worlds of philanthropy, education, art and medicine. The hospitals, museums, colleges and charitable institutions founded by the Parsi shipwrights who made their fortunes helping the British ship Indian opium to the Chinese, turning the latter into a nation of addicts and the East India Company into the world's largest drug cartel. She doesn't know about the next generation of Parsi industrialists who inherited the wealth amassed from opium, and then, to make themselves respectable, built public hospitals, art galleries, performing arts centres, theatres, universities, convocation halls, cancer treatment facilities, research institutes, drinking fountains, prayer halls, statues, and thousands of other services and structures. The midwife doesn't see the fine black residue on the nation's great buildings, railways and highways, on the scientists, engineers, doctors, musicians, painters and philosophers funded by tainted institutions, on the financial instruments that drive the stock market, on the knighthoods and other honours the founders acquire, on the automobiles and ships and airplanes they build, until it seems as if the nation has been founded on the forced addiction of millions of unfortunates whose need fuels an empire. The brutality of the business model. A product so certain of its effects that no one, no priest or soldier or parent, was immune to its call.

The midwife takes opium twice a day in a drink she calls *karrap*, which it is, *black* as her true love's heart, a lump of resin she mixes into hot water and sips, equal parts pleasure and pain. Married at fifteen to a toddy-tapper who started sipping arrack on the morning of the wedding and didn't stop for the three years their marriage lasted. When the dowry her parents paid his family turned out to be half the promised ten thousand rupees, her husband beat her, joyfully, efficiently, boasting to his friends about the black eyes and bruises he bestowed upon his wife. A year after the wedding when his friends joked about her childlessness, the beatings grew worse. A pestle left a scar on her forehead. She lost a tooth. Then the beatings stopped. Her husband grew thinner and weaker, his bones brittle. The doctor said he had the wasting disease, and in a year her husband died while she looked to be glowing. The villagers said it was no disease, it was Karrap. They named her after her opium habit, but the name was a veiled insult that held a double meaning. She was a husband-killer, a poisoner adept at the black arts. Expert at setting bones with wooden splints wrapped in herb-soaked bandages, at removing warts with a length of horsehair, at inducing abortions with the aid of a vile home-made tonic. She was to be found on full moon nights at the cemetery, collecting soil from the graves of dead children. Someone had seen her at Poojappura Central Prison, where she bribed her way past the high walls to harvest mandragoras that grew where a hanged man had ejaculated. Where Azhakeshan the Ripper was hanged, she came away with a sack full of mandrakes that had unusually long taproots and flowers so violet that the potion she concocted was more poisonous than any she'd made before. The only thing known about her with any certainty: unable to have children of her own, she delivered other women's babies and never married again. Her husband was the only man she had known. Dead as he was, poisoned or not, she loved him and always would.

In the birthing room, as the hours pass, unease slips past the curtain that veils Karrap's eyes.

'Scissoran,' she says, 'she needs a scissoran delivery. Any hospital can do it. Even now you can send for a doctor from Alwaye.'

The house is on the banks of the Muvattupuzha River, two miles from the main road of the small village of Mamalassery. The nearest hospital is half a day by road, or an hour by boat. Neither is an option.

'It's too late to bring a doctor,' Chachiamma says.

'Head. Too big,' Karrap mutters. She looks closely into Chachiamma's face and sees the determination there, something immovable. There's no use insisting on a doctor.

As night falls, the labour seems to become more difficult, as if the baby's head is growing in the womb, growing by the minute into something monstrous that will destroy the mother.

'Push,' Karrap says. 'Push, daughter.'

Ammu regrets everything that happened to her, the charming, bearded stranger, the letters they exchanged, falling into love and marriage. Most of all, she regrets getting pregnant. Nothing is worth this pain. She hears her mother say the same thing the Karrap woman is saying. And she does it, she pushes and pushes again and nothing happens. The baby doesn't move.

'Like that,' says Chachiamma. 'Just push.'

Ammu says, 'I don't want to push. I don't want anything.'

'Yes, girl,' says Chachiamma, 'I felt the same way nine times!'

But it's a lie to make her daughter feel better. Her childbirths were nothing like this. Ammu's fingers are laced around the bars of the headboard. Her eyes bulge, streaming with tears, her small, hard feet dance on the bed. For a moment, she stops breathing. When the scream comes, it is a bloodless shriek. Chachiamma's neck prickles. Even the midwife moans in fear. Ammu goes on and on until she is out of breath and the scream breaks up into sobs and coughing. Chachiamma is praying in a mix of Aramaic and Sanskrit, the broken and patched-together language in which the Sunday service is conducted. She has memorized the hour-long recitation, and now the words came unbidden.

'Deyvamey shudham olavan avunnu.'

Ammu hears the words as another part of the strangeness gathered around the object in her belly. Years later, at a Pentecostal service, when a congregation of devotees speak in tongues, she will remember her mother's mysterious birthing prayers.

Towards dawn, there is a thud in the yard. A kadukachi, she thinks. No, a sign. Soon, her ordeal will be over. The wind roars through the trees. She hears the crack of a heavy branch and a muffled thud as it falls to the ground. Another downpour is coming.

'Marnam elaathevanney shudham olavan avunnu.'

The bloodless scream comes again, but louder. She pushes and shouts and clutches her mother's hand. The midwife covers her ears, this woman who has induced so many abortions and guided so many births.

And still the baby does not move.

'Barachimo, slomo, barachimo, slomo.'

The prayer has become gibberish. In her distress, Chachiamma has forgotten the order. She's never been sure of the meaning of the words memorized without understanding, only fervour. Now she says them any which way and it doesn't matter. They are a comfort.

Tired of Thomas's questions, she sends him to the rubber grove at first light. The trees are ready for tapping, she knows, and soon the latex sheets must be taken to the villages along the coast. Reluctantly, he poles the scull across the flooded fields to the grove, half an acre of rubber trees planted in precise rows. Each tree stands in its own puddle of water and bears incisions made at a sharp angle for maximum yield. Chachiamma leaves the birthing room for a moment to watch his tall figure under a palm-leaf umbrella hat poling towards the rubber grove. She couldn't know that she is standing in the exact spot at which, sixty-two years later, her granddaughter, also named Chachiamma, will hold her infant daughter and wait for a boat to make its way across the flooded fields, or that the man rowing the boat will be Ammu's baby who seems so reluctant to emerge into the world.

The small rain comes again, very small, a light patter on the big leaves of the banana trees. The birds start their clamour: it's too dark, too early. The thunder continues and the real rain begins. Like stones hurled against the tin roof of the boathouse. They hear cries from the river, people crossing to the opposite bank caught in the downpour.

For seconds at a time, lightning illuminates trees caught in that furious dance. The lowing of panicked cattle fills the air.

Thomas poles back through the storm, the scull weighted now with bunches of coconuts he has cut from the trees near the rubber grove. He pulls up on to a patch of high ground near the front porch and unloads them. Then he sits in the planter's chair and reads the newspaper. When he gets to the last page, he goes back to the first. Not knowing what to do with himself, he paces the floor, then picks up a towel and goes to the river as he does each morning. The smell of the river, the resistance of the water, the tug in the middle where the current is strongest, these things calm him. When he returns to his chair, he extends the leg-rests and stares out at the fields. The old well has held up against the rain, but its tile roof needs repair. He picks up the paper and reads the front page again. Protest rallies against Namboodiripad's popular government by anti-communist church organizations allied with the Congress party. The agitation's gathering or losing steam, depending on which side you believe. What shocks him is the suggestion that the Christian groups are funded by the CIA. How could it be? How unchristian of them. He turns to the inside pages and rereads the opinion columns for the second or third time, fully anxious now.

The baby does not emerge.

'Did you eat something?' Thomas asks his wife.

'Who can eat?'

'Chachi, other children have been born here, we always manage.'

'Never again,' says his wife. 'No more babies will be born in this house. I am writing it on my head! From now on, they go to hospital.'

TWENTY-TWO YEARS LATER, THOMAS, who's never been to a hospital and has never spent a night away from his own handmade teak bed, will come in after his river bath feeling unwell. An event in itself, since the old man has never been ill. (It becomes part of his story that, on the morning of his death at the unforeseeable age of ninety-three, he bathed in the river as he had done every morning of his life, whatever the weather.) His son Chellan arrives and says in his persuasive manner that they should go to the hospital. At that moment, the old man remembers his dead wife's words. *From now on, they go to hospital.* The face that has never been seen to smile softens. 'Yes,' he tells his son, 'but no injections, no tubes, no oxygen. When it's time, I'll go.' A palanquin is brought to take him from the house to the main road, a walk he has taken countless times with his staff in hand. He is transferred to Chellan's car and they drive to the hospital. Late that night, he asks for an achan. The first words out of his mouth in half a day. The resident priest is brought to his bedside and intones the lord's prayer. *Swargastanaaya nangalude pithaave, ninte naamam parishudham aakanameh ... ninte rajyam varanameh ...* ending with the word that Thomas repeats in his turn. *Ameen.* When the priest leaves, Thomas turns to Chellan.

'It's time,' he says.

He shuts his eyes and is true to his word. Images flare in his head, flare and slow and flare again, the first time he sees a car, uniformed driver at the wheel, archbishop in the back seat waving at the baffled villagers, among them his headmaster, grinning helplessly, front tooth missing, the title sequence of a Hindi movie, steam train pulling into a station, two riders pass a rocky bluff, *Sholay* in bright red letters in three languages, in the theatre cigarette smoke shot through with beams from the projection room, learning to milk a cow, the milk frothing in a pan, red and yellow CPI slogans on the mossy walls near the railway station, white hammer and sickle on the station porch, slowly, deliberately, Raju the kitchen boy cuts off a chicken's head, the bird spouts blood on the gravel, running in ever smaller circles, red bulbs shooting from its neck, not knowing it has died, knowing it has died, his first wife's unbending posture on the boat when he sent her back to her parents and lover across the river, she doesn't look back, not once, and for that he's grateful, his own face, unbending, unforgiving, self-punishing, the herd of wild buffalo in the blue hills above Wayanad, distant blue, bluer than the sky, old sludge when the monsoon failed and the river exposed its black intestines, whitened bones of the long-drowned, the look in Annie's eyes, brightness fading, fever radiating from her skin, imploring him, imploring her father, knowing she has died, Ammu's baby emerging at three-forty in the afternoon, eighteen and a half hours after labour began, Karrap's hands smeared with blood, the three women pouring sweat, cord cut, baby bathed and swaddled, the mother too exhausted to hold the newborn, Chachiamma taking it into her arms, the determined look on her face, the simple wooden cross in the main room of the house, their separate beds, Chachiamma's face waiting for him on the other side of time, and he watches the river seep into the floor of the hospital room, green water thick with weeds, mud, river detritus, his bed quickly submerged, the room filling with murky light, quickly completely submerged, and at the spot where the window was, a square of radiance glows ever brighter, glows until it fills his sight and everything is green.

THE CHILDREN ARE THREE AND FIVE when she sells the Cadell Road apartment and the family moves to Bihar. George takes a job as editor of *The Searchlight*. There are student riots against the government. When the newspaper speaks up for the students, the chief minister orders George's arrest. On his release, the family goes back to Bombay and he returns, briefly, to his old job. Ammu finds a two-bedroom apartment in Shirin Building, Colaba, larger than the Cadell Road house and closer to George's office at the *Free Press*.

The months progress into social chaos spiky with hallucinogens, a stoned parade of paisley shirts, chillums, sideburns, miniskirts, electric guitars, bongos, daytime jam sessions. As with all trends in the time before the internet, the sixties arrive in India five years late, which is to say, in the early seventies. Beat groups spring up like magic mushrooms, the names fragrant with hash and confusion: Atomic Forest, Synthetic Frost, Kosmic Junk, Dr Dong & the Wrinkled Scrotum, The Beat Ovens, Velvette Fogg, High, Devil Beats, De Void, Mystiks, The Lone Trojan, Voodoos, Remo and the Microwave Papadums ... At the same time, twenty years after Indian independence, a new nationalism makes foreigners out of neighbours. You don't have to be from the British Isles or Central Asia to be an outsider.

Ammu takes them to a sugar-cane stall. They are drinking iced cane juice when the vendor asks where they are from.

'You're not from here,' he says in Marathi.

'Do you know Malayalam?' her son asks in Malayalam.

The vendor gives him a look.

'If you are Madrasis living in Bombay, you should speak Marathi not Malayali,' he says.

'We're not from Madras and Malayali is not a language,' her son says in English. 'One more, please.'

The sugar-cane man's expression changes in an instant. Ammu, frightened, takes her children by the hand. All the way home she checks the street to see if they're being followed.

'How did he know we were not Maharashtrian?' she asks George. 'Is it because we're darker?'

'It's the new party, the Shiv Sena, very popular,' says George. 'They only care about the sons and daughters of the immediate soil. If you were born in another state, you're an outsider.'

'We're from here,' she says. 'How can we be outsiders?'

But she thinks of herself as someone from Anniethottam. The other places will come and go without leaving much of an impression. In Hong Kong or New York or Bombay or Bangalore, it is the news out of Kerala she will follow. She is a Malayali before she is a citizen of Elsewhere.

'When six people die in a flash flood in Cochin, you talk about it for days,' her son tells Ammu. 'Sixty people die in Bombay and you don't even notice.'

'Donkey,' she says. 'People die. That's what they do.'

'Unless they're Malayali, in which case it's a catastrophe.'

She gives it a moment of thought, shakes her head and says, 'You have to choose your place in the world.'

Over half a century later, Ammu and George will return to their chosen place, a return they've imagined time and again in the years they've been away. But by then, Kerala has changed and they have too. There is no sense of belonging or welcome. They've lived Elsewhere too long: they've become Elsewhereans.

He wakes early, thinking of the summer holidays and the two months of unsupervised adventure ahead of him. The elation dips when Ammu takes out swimwear for lessons at the pool. Lessons are lessons. They have no place during the holidays. He knows there's no use pointing out this important fact, but he does so anyway, with the expected result. His mother says it has been decided. As if the decision has been taken by the highest authority and cannot be changed.

At ten, they walk to the Afghan Church bus stop and wait until a double-decker BEST bus creakily arrives, then go up to the front seat on the top deck. He calls out the stops as if he were the conductor.

'First stop, Colaba Post Office.'

Ammu watches as her daughter, two years younger, repeats the words to herself. She is her brother's opposite, quiet, averse to trouble, obedient, unless he's convinced her to take part in some hare-brained scheme. In temperament, she is older and wiser.

There is a squeal of ancient brakes.

'Second stop, Colaba Bus Station.'

The bus fills. Behind them, a group of students discuss examinations, tutorials and college seats reserved for the underprivileged. There is talk of unfair advantage and the death of meritocracy. On the other side of the aisle, two navy men in uniform sit stiffly upright, staring out the front window.

'Third stop, Sassoon Dock,' says her son.

'Sassoon Dock, Fire Brigade Centre,' corrects his sister, reading the sign in its entirety.

The smell of fish is around them, fried fish, sun-dried fish, the pungency of rotten fish. So strong a smell, a person could faint, thinks Ammu. From her seat, she has a view of the entrance to the market, and she notes the women going in, saris hiked between their buttocks, on their heads baskets of glistening fish. They come out with empty baskets, talking in high-pitched voices, heads bobbing, as loud and unrestrained as men. She envies their ease and sense of belonging.

'Fourth stop, Strand Cinema.'

Slowly, the smell of fish recedes, very slowly, like a curtain lifting, and petrol fumes and exhaust take its place. A horse carriage cuts them off, in the seat a group of Arab women covered from head to toe, eyes hidden behind leather masks. The bus driver sounds his horn as the traffic backs up. It sets off a chorus of honks.

'Fifth stop, Regal Cinema.'

As he says aloud the name of each stop, her son writes them down in a red notebook. The roundabout comes into view, and Ammu points out the road that leads to the Bombay Port Trust where their father once applied for a job in the merchant navy. George was new to Bombay and working at the *Free Press*. The only post he could find was that of a cook on a merchant ship. He travelled around the world and wrote a book about it.

'What was the name of the ship?' asks her son.

'SS *Jalakanya*,' says Ammu.

He writes the name in the notebook and puts it back in his pocket, a mannerism copied from his father.

'Is that why he took a job on a ship, to write about it?'

'To see the world *and* write about it. He likes to travel. It's something we have in common.'

'Why do you like to travel?'

'Excuse me, madam,' says a new voice. 'May I say something?'

It is one of the navy men sitting across from them, a slight man in his mid-thirties. Ammu nods, too startled to reply.

'I fear it's something we're born with. From the moment we can walk, we want to see things we haven't seen before. We promise ourselves we'll go here or there. So, when we're abroad, walking past a fountain or a piazza, we're keeping a promise to our past selves, maybe made in a past life. Our hope is to remember in the end but half of what we have seen.'

Her son breaks the silence that follows.

'Did you join the navy to see the world?'

'I could have joined the army, there also you see the world,' says the man. 'But the navy has a *big* plus point.'

'You navigate by the stars?'

'That's a plus, you're quite right,' says the navy man, 'but I'm thinking of something more important than even the stars.'

'Tell!'

'In the navy, you don't have to shoot people.'

There is silence again as the boy considers the unquestionable advantages of not having to shoot someone. Then he stands up.

'Sixth stop, Electric House.'

They say goodbye to the navy and quickly make their way out of the bus. Ammu takes each child by the hand as they walk two blocks to the pool. There, on the first day of swimming lessons, she watches as her children demonstrate, repeatedly, how unsuited they are for the water. She is a champion swimmer from a family of champion swimmers. If she's disappointed, she keeps it to herself.

THEN COMES THE DAY THEY UNDERSTAND only later, long after what happened has happened, when they are able to piece together and connect the sequence of events that led to their parents disappearing in front of their eyes.

Ammu and George like to discuss their plans for the day. Even a drive to the city involves much comparing of one route over another. So, when they set off on a trip one morning with no prior discussion, or none that the children overhear, it is a special excitement. Ammu says they will stay with Uncle Baby for some time. Each child is given a suitcase in their favourite colour, red for the daughter and green for the son. Ammu and George have identical navy-blue cases. In the car, George is unusually silent while Ammu distractedly reaches over from the front seat to remake her daughter's braids and chatter about unrelated topics. How she should have paid closer attention to her mother's cooking and written down some of her recipes, how important it is to listen to one's elders, how glad she is that the hot weather has passed, how good it is that her youngest brother, Jacob, has returned to Mamalassery from Ethiopia because his wife, Uma, is pregnant again, how much she misses her mother's food, just as her children will one day miss hers, and then she talks of the navy officer on the bus and his idea that men and women are born to move.

'Correct, he was,' she says. 'Common sense. From the beginning, we wandered the earth. The old books are full of people on the move. Look at the Bible! Moses and Noah and Jesus never stopped moving around. The Iliad too, full of people with itchy feet, Ulysses and Achilles and all those other men whose names end with -es.'

'Well, travel is a constant in the Indian tradition too, in the Ramayana for instance,' says George. 'Rama, Sita and Lakshmana wandered around the forests for fourteen years. In the Mahabharata, exile lasts twelve years. Yudhishthira and his brothers and his wife cross the nation on foot and ascend the tallest mountain in the world. Along the way, one by one his family members are lost, until at the end the old king stands alone on the mountaintop, feeling no elation, only sorrow.'

In the back seat, the children consider this new information.

'Is that what you want to do?' asks the boy. 'Travel across the nation and climb the tallest mountain and see the world from the top?'

Ammu and George together say: 'Yes!' Later, they will remember the enthusiasm with which their parents had agreed.

In Mahim, George parks the car outside his brother's house. Ellie serves lunch in the front room on the table with its doilies and embroidered runner, then George and Baby step out for a cigarette.

'Why don't you show them the globe that Uncle Baby bought?' Ammu says to Ellie. 'Go on, you two, you'll see the route your father took when he was working on the ship. Bombay–Hamburg–Berlin–London–Newcastle. Make a note!'

Ellie leads the way into the bedroom to show them where exactly the cities are on the little spinning globe on the sideboard. By tracing the route from India to Germany to the United Kingdom, they see how daring the journey must have been, how much distance was covered, how audacious it was to travel across the sea and live for days and weeks on the perilous water. The boy goes out to ask his father how long the voyage had taken, so as to make a note of it for the day when he will make a similar adventure. Through the open front door, he sees movement, his parents in the car, Uncle Baby driving. They are already halfway down the street. He catches sight of his mother in the back seat, the two navy-blue cases beside her.

Ellie Auntie stops him from running after them.

'Where are they going?'

And that's how he comes to know that his parents are flying off on their own adventure.

CHICKEN KIEV

Hanoi, 1973 | Hong Kong, 1975 | Bangalore, 2017

Or a narrator who can't distinguish between present and past and future. Who lives in a home for the elderly, or a minimum-security prison, or a rehab centre, or a cottage on the grounds of an insane asylum. Who begins each chapter with a falsified claim or quote, e.g., For a long time, I went to bed early … to watch television.

WILD METAL MUSIC IN THE STREETS of Hong Kong, electric screech of napalm, monks on fire, screaming horses. Nightly brawls in Central and Wanchai. People from all over the world roam the island, squaddies, sailors, bankers, spies, drug dealers, con artists, all kinds of adventurers looking for booze and trouble. 1967, Year of the Fire Sheep, the Age of Aquarius and Vietnam.

Fifty years later, he tells his son of his Hanoi adventure. It is unusual to hear stories from George's past. Father and son aren't close.

In his late teens and early twenties in Madras and Bombay, George aligns himself with the student communist movement. Years later, while working in Hong Kong, Raghavan, a friend from his days in Bombay, offers to arrange a visit to North Vietnam. (Journalists from Western publications aren't allowed into the north.) Raghavan is a known communist and a correspondent for *Blitz*, the tabloid of the Indian independence movement. Unexpectedly, he'd accepted an invitation to George's wedding and they've been in touch ever since.

'This was in 1972 or 1973,' George says. 'Every journalist worth his salt wanted to get into Hanoi. They'd never have let me in, but Raghavan vouched for me. I have no idea why. We had our disagreements.'

'What about?'

'After Stalin and Mao, I cooled a little. He would talk about Che and I'd counter with Isaac Babel.' A bit of the old bounce returns to his voice. 'He didn't give in, neither did I.'

'You hit an impasse.'

'Actually, it was a huge surprise to hear from him.'

North Vietnam considers India a friendly nation, so the trip has to be arranged from Delhi. George flies in from Hong Kong and meets up with Raghavan. Together, they take an Air India flight to Hanoi. For the next few months, he files stories about what people say and what they wear, how they live, what they eat, how much or how little they sleep, stories about women as equal partners in the building of the nation, about sustainability and the environment before these topics become the fashion.

'What I wanted was to concoct a potted spiritual history.'

'Not sure what that means, spiritual history?'

'As in, describe how a material object, say a bowl of soup, or a hammock, or a wristwatch, might affect someone's spirit.'

'Well, go on,' says his son, drawn in. It is as if, after a lifetime of silence, George has discovered conversation.

'Objects have an inner life acquired from the people to whom they're attached. I thought it might be possible to describe a society by describing the things it uses, grand objects as well as humble ones, especially humble ones.' He is talking about humility, but there is a hint of pride. 'You can tell a lot by looking at a water canteen used by a soldier in a presidential motorcade. Or a small, propeller-driven airplane full of chickens and bicycles. If you study the way a pulverized bridge is rebuilt ... Objects tell stories. I thought, if I found the right ones, I could recount...'

He stops and stares into the distance. Then he goes to the storeroom off the kitchen and his son follows. George looks into the drawers of half a dozen file cabinets in which he's saved the documents and sundry keepsakes he brought back from his trips, as well as household materials, tax receipts, property papers. His son knows the cabinets well. He's looked through them many times for clues to those years. The drawers are deep and crowded. George fishes out all kinds of things, examines them at length, then puts them back where he found them. Official invitations, photographs and postage stamps. Newspaper cuttings. Chopsticks, bowls and teapots. Coins and banknotes. An ornate buffalo-horn comb. He hands over shredded notebooks held together by thick rubber bands, some notes in a mixture of Malayalam and English. Some entries ticked, some not. When his son asks why, George says a tick indicates the note has been used in a report he filed. His son is dismayed at how many have never been used. George keeps searching and finds a peaked cap with a yellow star on the band, red and yellow silk flags, perfectly preserved, Ho Chi Minh propaganda posters, not so well preserved.

'Here it is,' he says, holding up a black-and-white photograph, a woman on a motorcycle looking into the camera.

'Who's this?'

'Nguyen Phuc Chau, our manager on those trips.'

'I remember the name. It's in your journals. A lot.'

'We wanted to see what it looked like, the border between south and north. Really difficult to get permission, but somehow she fixed it up. She told us to have a heavy breakfast. Long drive. We might not eat for a while. It turned out to be not difficult at all. I asked why she tried to frighten us. I honestly wanted to know. You know what she said?'

'I'm sure I don't.'

'That's how she was trained. From childhood. Always to be ready for disaster. The remark stayed with me, and even now I can recall the tone of voice in which she said it.'

There are clues to all this in George's Vietnam notebooks. This passage in particular:

> *Left Hanoi 8 a.m. They sent 2 jeeps ahead – one with petrol, the other with 200 kgs worth of food including a 100 bottles of beer and 1/2 doz baskets of live chickens. Wondered why this waste. But the wisdom of it dawned on me as we bumped our way from hazard to hazard on the way to the 17th Parallel.*
>
> *At Ben Thuy ferry in Vinh got word that a pontoon bridge had been disrupted by storm. So turned back and stayed the night. Though capital, the city's been badly crippled by bombing. Rather primitive living conditions at best guest house. Life revolved around a well from which you drew water.*
>
> *About 11 next morning, got word bridge was open. But progressed hardly 30 km when we had to stop. It was out of commission again and 2 km of trucks had lined up. Heavy duty trucks laden with tyres, petrol in cans, boats, pigs, steel rails, crates of unknown goods.*
>
> *After hrs of waiting at this causeway amidst paddy, we walked to the bridge, crossed it and found another jeep coming for us. Our manager Nguyen Phuc Chau had found a telephone – in that desolate paddy expanse she could get Hanoi and 17th Parallel towns in 10 or 15 minutes – contacted the administration in Ha Tinh and arranged for a pick-up.*

She had said nothing of it, told us we'd have to walk 10 km to the nearest guest house near Ha Tinh – and that's what Raghavan and I set out to do. When the jeep picked us up, I asked Nguyen Phuc Chau why she didn't tell us it was coming. She said: to keep your morale high.

I've never seen Raghavan happier than in the midst of a ruined countryside among people who won't accept ruin as their destiny.

Thanks to Nguyen Phuc Chau's resolve we reached Ha Tinh guest house. From main road a dust track through marsh and paddy branched off through fields until we reached an enclave set amidst pine and banana trees. Why a guest house in this far-off place, I asked. This is one of our evacuation sites, said Nguyen Phuc Chau. Idyllic cluster of huts, overrun by frogs, resounding with the croak of crickets. The girls managing it greeted us with a warm 'Chao Dong Chi' and gave a sumptuous dinner. But, for breakfast, no bread or even noodles. We were too cut off.

After the fall of Saigon, George teaches journalism at a school in the north. It is supposed to be a four-week trip, but he is away much longer. Ammu tells the children he is making up his mind whether or not to start a school. They know it is more than a question of making up his mind. How long could that take? As the weeks go by, they become convinced he isn't coming back. It is abandonment, plain and simple. His mind is on other, more important things, politics, ideas, the future not the past. In those days, while he is gone and they aren't sure when he'll return, Ammu seems to catch George's lifelong condition.

'Who knows,' brother tells sister, 'maybe it's contagious.'

'What is?'

'Like chickenpox. Spreads on contact.'

'Yeah, but what?'

'Silence. Maybe she's caught it.'

Ammu says little, but the strain is evident on her face and in her distracted, uncertain manner. Mealtimes become erratic. Because she forgets to eat, she forgets the children need to eat. If they ask for something, she tells them to get it themselves, they are old enough. She leaves tasks undone or half-done, when she has always insisted that leaving something half-done was just the same as not doing it at all. Long past dinnertime, they find rice soaking in a pan, as if she's forgotten to put it in the pressure cooker or lost interest altogether. They find a half-peeled cucumber on the cutting board, the peeler flung to the side. Some mornings, they find her asleep on the dining table as if she's been awake all night. Softly her son says, 'Mama?' And she gets hurriedly to her feet and hugs them and gets them ready for school.

'What's wrong with her?'

'Nothing. Nothing's wrong. It's a phase, that's all.'

Seven months after he leaves, George returns. But his high spirits are gone. He is a new, subdued man. Ammu greets him formally. There is no shouting or recrimination, or none that can be heard. Often at night and sometimes in the day, there are polite, low-pitched conversations. And after these marital councils, husband and wife look solemn, not angry or sorrowful. George goes back to work. Ammu starts to take an interest in the house and in her children. Between them there is silence, where earlier there has been conversation and laughter. Then this period ends, and it ends like this:

'We're going to the Press Club,' Ammu says after George has come home from work and before he changes his clothes. 'For dinner.'

'What?'

'I didn't cook today. I didn't feel like it. Make sure you're carrying enough money.'

'I am. I mean, I will.'

'I want the Chicken Kiev.'

'But you call it the butter bomb.'

'That's what I want.'

'Me too,' say the children in unison.

'Okay, then,' says George.

'I'll get these two ready. We'll leave in half an hour.'

Years afterwards, when George speaks of Vietnam and its people, it is with gratitude and affection. By then, his son has put things together and come up with a theory. He asks when George had last seen Nguyen Phuc Chau.

'Probably 1986. She wanted to move south to Saigon and conduct tours of the city.'

'Not really?'

'To administer a corrective. Her words, not mine.'

'Correct whom?'

'Tourists who treated her country as if it were a culture to be consumed. Peeping tourists. Again, her words.'

'The world's economies depend on them.'

There is a pause while he weighs how much to say. Then:

'I wanted to go on one of those tours, but it was not to be. She must be an old lady now. Sometimes you miss people, you wonder what became of them. If you go to Vietnam, remember me to her. She was very important to me in those days.'

'You've spoiled it,' says his son. 'You shouldn't have said that. It's better to be silent about some things.'

Nothing is said for a moment.

'You like to have the last word, don't you?' says George.

'No, I don't. I don't like to have the last word.'

A family code has been abandoned for no good reason. Silence is a lesson his son has learned. Now George has changed a fundament, replaced tradition with its opposite – at his whim. His son feels betrayed. But in a moment, his resentment is gone, replaced by satisfaction. It is true after all, the near-miss his sister and he had imagined. It was an actual family crisis that Ammu had managed all by herself. Who knows how narrowly its full extent had been averted?

In the notebooks, a wealth of clues and stories. Written as a series of pictures, sprinkled throughout with novelistic detail, from a time when George still had hopes of writing a novel.

16-7-73
Air trip Dong Hoi–Hanoi

Thought our jeep driver was going to wrong end of airfield. But wasn't; the tent was the check-in and reception, and all. Benches, tea, and publications hanging on a rope.

Aircraft parked on lawn. Under its shade some 10 people. Around, some 40 cows.

Man asked local people to go to board. A group which I thought had come to see the plane went ahead with their pies, bundles, cycles.

The cycles too boarded. Another guy with singlet went around aircraft looking at it: flight engineer.

Delay of some minutes. Thought they were clearing the cows. Then saw a group of 6 coming from another corner of the field. Oh, new passengers, I thought. No, that was the crew. Bush shirt & trousers. Two hostesses, no [illegible] is only difference. No insignia, uniform. Then we boarded. Spacious comfortable cabin. Excellent flight. Luggage taken up and kept at rear of cabin. At Hanoi, hostesses helped bring them down.

But his son's mind is on another passage from the notes.

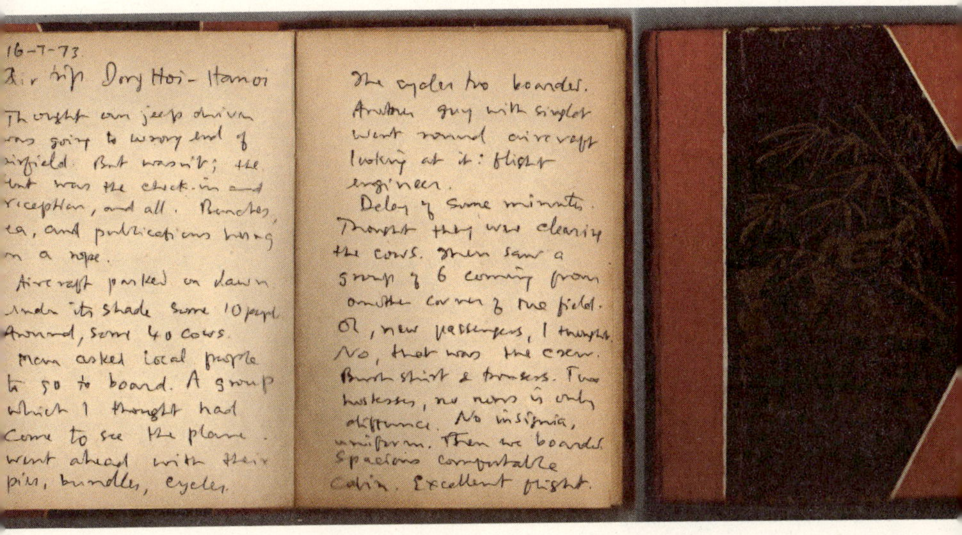

When the jeep picked us up, I asked Nguyen Phuc Chau why she didn't tell us it was coming. She said: to keep your morale high.

When he gets the chance, he flies to Vietnam, hoping to find someone last seen three decades earlier. She may have died or changed her name or moved to another country. All he has is a business card and a photograph.

His morale, admittedly, is not high.

WOMAN ON A MOTORCYCLE

Saigon to Hanoi, 2018

'I knew that he respected the Vietcong and their North Vietnamese allies as the greatest soldiers in the greatest army thus far in the twentieth century.'

WALTER MOSLEY, ***Blood Grove***

'I HATE VIETNAM,' SAYS THE WOMAN in the window seat. 'My father died in the last days of the war. One more week, and he would have been stateside. Vietcong shot him right in the back. We didn't get much of him except his uniform. Try talking to a uniform sometime, try telling your troubles to an empty sleeve. Then I find out he had kids here, two daughters.' She clasps her arms around herself. 'My half-siblings, I guess you could call them. I hate Vietnam, and you can't rightly blame me.'

M says, 'Why go?'

'What do you mean, why go?'

'If you hate it, why?'

'Hey, to meet my half-sisters, for the first and only time, I'm betting.'

M shrugs, as if to suggest it might be a good thing.

'Oh, and I hate the rain,' the woman says, 'because then I hear his voice and I know he's trying.'

'Wait, I don't understand. Trying what?'

'To tell me something,' she says, spreading her dry, pale hands, sure of her place in the world. 'He's saying, take the next flight home. Get the hell out of Dodge, pronto. Goodnight, Vietnam.'

She clasps herself once more. There is a satin scrunchie around her wrist, blonde hair caught in the folds. Her nails are painted white.

'Wait,' she says. 'You're not Vietnamese, are you?'

M shakes her head.

From the aisle seat, I have to peer across M and the woman. My first view of Vietnam is rain flattened against the aircraft's small windows, the droplets moving upwards as we lose altitude. Below us, farmland dissected by a great road that winds back into itself in the shape of the numeral eight, a silver infinity symbol that gleams against the darkness of the fields. The plane bucks and the engine hum shifts gears. Someone gasps. Seat belt signs come on. For a moment the ground seems above us, then the scene rights itself and I see that the roadway in the shape of infinity is a glowing river that restores the landscape through which it flows – the socialist republic narrow as a corridor or a strip of coastline, impervious to conquest. The woman is silent now. Zigzag rain shadows move across her face as she examines the country below her. Quietly, hoping she won't hear, I say to M that at moments like this air travel is a kind of time travel: we fly into a new time zone and put ourselves back together on a cellular level. M says the theory only applies to long flights, where jet lag is really time lag. It's why frequent flyers age so fast, they are constantly recalibrating, sometimes in one direction and then in the other. 'It makes for a lot of psychic wear and tear,' says M, 'but I live in Australia and that means getting anywhere is an eight- or nine-hour flight up from the bottom of the world. Bangkok to Saigon, ninety minutes or less, doesn't qualify as a flight in my opinion, it's a hop, nothing more.'

'Australia?' says the woman in the window seat. 'I've never been. I can't understand the language. I mean, I know it's English, but I can't. You I understand. You don't sound Australian.'

'I don't know what to say to that,' says M.

'Well,' says the woman, 'where are you really from?'

M thinks about it for a moment and says, 'I'm from anywhere.'

As she says *anywhere*, the wheels hit the runway and the plane bounces. Here we go, I think, M is right, this isn't moving forward or backward but sideways, a lateral move into some place where time is almost the same, almost.

As usual when flying, because I take pills for anxiety, I don't recall how we get to the hotel from the airport, the traffic or lack of traffic, the paperwork while checking in. I remember changing rooms to one on a lower floor, which is slightly more spacious and slightly less noisy. And I remember sitting at the window that night and looking through my father's Vietnam notebooks, although I have no recollection the next day of copying some passages into my own book, ending with these lines:

> *Chairman: Dinh Quang Nghi: 49. Olive green ~~military~~ shirt. Blue trousers. Ho Chi Minh sandals. Couple of gold teeth. Stalky [sic]. Takes out of trouser pocket wristwatch he kept wrapped in hanky.*

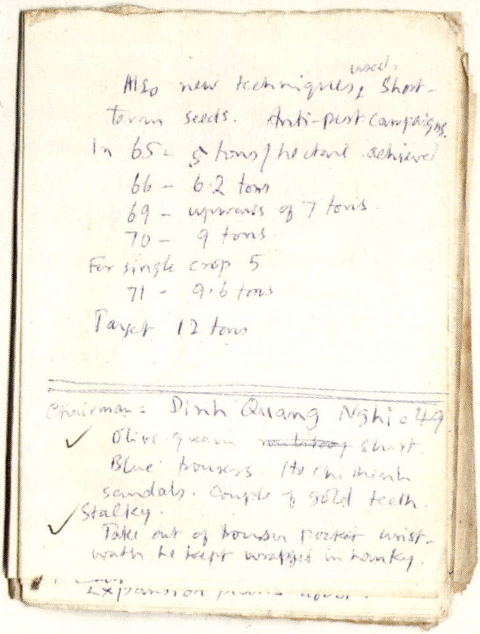

In my mind, Chairman Nghi comes to anxious life. I see him retrieve the handkerchief-wrapped watch, which he keeps in his pocket to save it from daily wear. With a few phrases, a fully formed personality has stepped off the page. I recognize the writer's eye at work – the word *military* cancelled because *olive green* is enough – and I am saddened that my father never wrote the novel he'd hoped to write. He became T.J.S. George, editor and political commentator, wasting his gift on newspapers. Nestled among the pages telling of the journey in which he met Chairman Nghi, is the photograph of the woman on a motorcycle, an image I'd seen first as a boy. Over the years, it has acquired for me the true quality of sepia, a moment from a vanished time that holds a message for the future. It has everything to do with why I am in Vietnam.

Sometimes you miss people, you wonder what became of them.

But my clearest memory of our arrival in Saigon is not of my father, or the woman in the photograph, or the mysterious connection between them. I remember rain boiling on the sidewalk, a car passing, headlights tunnelling through the dark, a woman in a leopard-skin turban and fringed leather vest crossing the street, her cigarette dry in the rain. She steps off the curb, trips lightly over her feet and stops to take off her high heels. Barefoot, she resumes her unhurried walk towards me. A garbage truck passes. When I look again, she is gone. I put my head out to check the sidewalk. There is only rain turned magenta by neon signage.

She wore it every chance she got. Alive or dead or in the thousand places in between. Soft, tan leather with a fringe of fine strips that hung from the waist to the knees and swayed when she swayed. He'd found it at a vintage store on St Mark's Place. Such a fit, like it was custom-made. Even now, in the half-here half-there world she'd created for herself with her own two hands and her restless unwise feet. Performed such sudden violence upon her person that she hadn't fully left the world. Was still in it. Still happy to sashay in the rain in her leather vest and blow his fucking mind. What did she remember? A shred here, a number there. Dry heat. Ceiling fan. Soundlessness. April 1, All Fool's Day. Why she did it, she couldn't say. Some trivial thing. A tiny leap backwards for womankind. A small step for woman. She stepped off the desk and tried not to struggle and remembered the girl at boarding school, the one she'd bullied. The children in their white pinafores like dead girls miming a vision of the end. All in white but for the ribbons. Frayed red satin sifting in the breeze. This is the worst night of my life, she said. But it was nothing, a night like any other. The end of a certain phase of being, not so different from the one before and the one before that. The world of innocence had left her the moment she joined the school as a child. The sweet world had never returned. In her vision of the dead girls in white, the angel of the end stood over them rejoicing at his meticulous handiwork. When his eyes came to her, they filled at first with glee and then with sudden tears. She understood the glee. He'd done his job and done it well. The tears were a mystery. 'Don't cry, baby,' she said. 'Everything's going to be all right. Silence is best, don't you know?'

It is still raining at dawn when I look for the shoes she flung aside, no longer certain I've seen what I've seen. I know I won't find them and I look anyway. The welt-coloured sky holds a yellow sliver of moon above the ramshackle buildings crowding the dead street. Rain thunders on the patio's awning and stone tiles. I remember what the woman on the flight said. I am in thrall to the rain, but if there are voices inside, I don't understand them. I tell M that I saw my wife the night before. Taken aback, for a moment she doesn't know what to say. But then it comes to her. The contract of good sense.

'You took two pills before the flight. Pills and wine. Have you looked up the side effects?'

The rain has thinned to a drizzle by breakfast. I place a call from reception. The man who answers has no English, and when I ask for Nguyen Phuc Chau – the name on the business card clipped to a photograph of someone George had met almost fifty years earlier – the phone is handed to a woman. I repeat my question, saying all three names for respect, as my father instructed. The woman answers with a question of her own. Where am I staying?

She says in her brisk American accent that our hotel is in District Four. 'Four is like island surrounded by water,' she says. 'All you have to do? Take taxi across Ben Nghe canal to District One. Tell taxi driver to take Calmette Bridge and it will bring you straight to our office.'

'What kind of office am I looking for?'

'But I thought you knew,' says the voice, 'this is travel agency started by my grandmother many years before.'

'May I speak with Nguyen Phuc Chau?'

'Before I answer, maybe you come here. Now, okay? Ask for Dana.'

I put the phone down and tell M the sequence of events that has brought us here, the photo in my father's files of a woman on a Saigon street in 1973. That her name was Nguyen Phuc Chau and she'd been the government-appointed guide when he reported on the war as a young journalist. That the number I just called was on her business card, which she gave him when they met again in 1986. M holds the photograph to the reading lamp on the bedside table. I can tell that she too is struck by the image of the confident young woman with the joyous smile, the World War II motorcycle she rides so casually, the denim bell-bottoms and open-toed sandals. Her hair has been carelessly cut and the fringe has grown out. And there is the man to the left of the frame watching George as he takes the photograph. Who is he, casual onlooker, jealous associate, North Vietnamese spy? 'I've wanted to meet the woman on the motorcycle ever since I was a boy,' I say. 'At last it seems possible.'

We set off along a street of appliance stores, the sidewalk crowded with scooters and plastic chairs. Green shuttered storefronts fly the national flag in all sizes, the bright yellow star against a field of red silk. On an avenue where families recline on straw mats spread among caged roosters and shops that sell table fans and ice coolers and wholesale coffee, we find a line of waiting taxis.

'I Googled the meds you take to fly,' M says in the cab. 'Ambien is a hypnotic. Hallucinations are a common side effect. You're meant to sleep, not mix it with alcohol. No wonder you saw things that weren't there.'

The sun was out and the woman I'd seen stumbling in the rain was far away: I let it be.

Calmette Bridge and neighbourhood are correctly named, an oasis of calm in comparison to Bui Vien and Pham Ngu Lao, the backpacker destinations we pass. The taxi drops us at a glass-fronted business that takes up the ground floor of a city block, NGUYEN TRAVELS emblazoned above the door. A security guard points to a young woman at a central desk. Her short hair falls in a heavy fringe to horn-rimmed glasses, the kind of haircut worn by schoolchildren. A row of metal chairs faces her, but she doesn't invite us to sit.

'You can call me Dana,' she says. 'My name is Da Nang, but call me Dana if it will be easier for you.'

I resolve to call her Da Nang. She says she is taking a small group to the Cu Chi tunnels and she'll give us a good price if we want to come along. But we must decide quickly, people are waiting.

We take seats on a bus with a dozen tourists. Two American families, a young Asian in designer sportswear, a group of Germans discussing *mittagessen* and *mittagsschlaf*. Da Nang is at the front, facing us, her sharp words belied by a friendly smile. I will discover that her friendliness is close to contempt. It helps make up for the shortcomings of her fellows. She begins with the greeting that now seems a bit of sarcasm, a bit of friendly contempt in her default American accent.

'Call me Dana. My name is Da Nang but you better not say it. Say Dana. It's easier, am I right? I can tell by looking at you it's easier. Do you know what happen when North and South Vietnam became one country after American War? Ah, some confusion. You are in Vietnam. The angle of perception is different here compared to eight thousand miles to the west. We did not start the war, we only ended it, we did not invade France and America, we only defeated them after they invaded us. So, what you call Vietnam War, we call…?'

Here, she pauses and looks at us.

Someone says, 'American War?'

'Yes, well done, American War,' says Da Nang. 'After American War, if you are from the north, if your family is communist, then free school, free education, free medical. You are taken care of your whole life. But if you are from Saigon? Then you pay because you are loser. You cannot marry policeman or government official. You can only marry other loser like you. Our government always say republics fail, only socialist countries can succeed. When will it succeed, we ask. One day, they say, be patient, you'll see. But we still waiting.'

Someone asks if she isn't afraid to be so outspoken.

'Sometimes, our government send police in plain clothes, but they are so obvious, minute I see them, I know.' She pauses, and the smile appears again, at odds with the suppressed anger of her speech. 'My auntie lives in the United States. She used to work for American during war. Twenty years later, American allow her to emigrate.'

'What about you,' asks a young German.

'I'm in no hurry to work in New Jersey nail salon. I am third-generation Saigonese, my grandmother was interpreter and guide who started agency after war.'

'Do you travel out of the country yourself?'

'If you want travel abroad, you must have fifty thousand dollars in bank account, otherwise you not allowed. So when we see tourists like you, we always think, oh, you are so rich, you have so much money to spend on holiday. Now we don't think like that. We know you not rich. Sometimes you more poor than us, or maybe you stingy.'

'You work for a travel agency and you don't travel?'

'I go near old Ho Chi Minh trail to Hanoi and from there to mountain once, maybe twice a year. There you find real Vietnam. But Saigon is my permanent living place.'

'Why?'

'Because,' the word is blurted, a full accusation, charged with anger against herself and the young man who asks, 'many of my family die in this city. I feel they still here. I feel they don't want to be alone.'

There are no more questions.

An hour and a half after we set out, the bus stops at the entrance to the tunnels. Tickets are purchased. There is a compulsory propaganda film of clumsy anti-Americanism. Then come photo and retail opportunities. The country has unified under the communist flag, but as with most former communists, money is the new ideology. We are taken to a captured American tank beached on a mound of yellow sand. Broken barrel pointing downwards, treads leaking rust. The Americans from our group and some of the Germans take turns to pose atop the turret.

When we regroup, Da Nang is smiling. I know what the smile means. She says that in the village of Cu Chi, more than a thousand American soldiers had died, mostly shot in the back. She says it casually, but an electric silence follows. She says, 'Vietminh hide in jungle, hide in bunkers under the ground, come out to shoot American. But not all American die from gunshot to back, some also die in Vietminh trap like this one. You see?' We see a rectangle of jungle grass the size of a large welcome mat. A young man in fatigues and a floppy camouflage hat peels back the mat to reveal a pit about four feet deep, planted with bamboo stakes sharpened to fine points. 'Some don't die,' says Da Nang, 'they only lose leg or other part. Vietminh very clever with bamboo.'

At a covered stand, the man in fatigues takes up the commentary.

'The tunnels stretch more than seventy-five miles,' he says blandly, 'interconnecting tunnels dug with our bare hands using only small tools. Tunnels that go all the way to Cambodia border. Everything you can imagine underground, hospitals, living quarters, kitchens, factories to make weapons, hammocks to have a good sleep, the whole network bomb-proof, this is *engineering marvel*. Now I'll show you another one.' He squats beside a barrel-like object with a concealed handle. As he turns, spikes mesh into each other from two sides. 'This is the rollin' trap. Rollin', rollin', rollin' on the river,' he sings. His powerful baritone transforms a steamboat shanty into the anthem of a river out of myth, the Mississippi, the Mekong, the Ganga, the Styx, a river in the Old Testament. 'And this is the door trap,' he says, 'when you open, ouch, some spikes appear in your lower body. No more happy endings!' He pauses while photographs are taken. 'And this one, this is the fish trap, very easy to get in, very hard to get out.' He goes on in this way, joyfully demonstrating traps of all kinds.

When we leave the covered embankment, those among us who have posed on the tank or by the door trap are talking in whispers, and although it is a sunny afternoon and the morning's rain drips moisture from the rubber trees, the atmosphere among our party has changed and darkened.

Da Nang leads us to the first of the tunnels, a hole just wide enough for a slender figure. She says, 'One thousand American died at Cu Chi.' She allows the number to take root in the imagination. 'But one hundred and fifty-five thousand Vietnamese died here. Dead American important to you, dead Vietnamese important to us. Who is right? Who knows? We learn one thing. Never again to let you come here. To be honest, we feel like we don't want tourist to come here either. Stay in your own country. Don't come! Okay, lecture finished, time to go into ground.'

We descend on rough steps carved into the earth, two short flights, and then into a hidden anteroom. I am behind M and ahead of a large man who will be in trouble if the tunnel narrows. We start off at a slow crawl, and in minutes the claustrophobia is upon me. I feel it on the concrete and in the air, heat residue left by thousands of bodies. Someone strains to breathe. There is the scrape of boot against bone. I shut my eyes and breathe through my nose and imagine we are out of the tunnel in the clean sunlight above. The fantasy lets me push away the sensation that I am deep underground and going ever deeper. But a voice puts my fear into words. 'I can't go on,' says the man behind me, the words a rasp in his throat. His five-year-old daughter, who is ahead of M, says, very calmly, that he has to keep going, there are people behind him and there is no other way out. More crawling. A smell of old sweat and testosterone. And then we are inside a mesh of shadows, light filtering through a forest of dust, bright in the middle and dimly dispersed at the bottom and sides, as if all brightness has been absorbed by those who have passed before us. For a moment, I see a vast vaulted room with pillared barricades on each side. Stone ladders lead up into the gloom. On each step, small children strain to reach the rung above them. I think I see more figures, tiny and bereft, hoping to gain the high maze-like partitions. But the heights are beyond reach and the small figures will strain this way forever. We crawl on and the barricades melt into the dark and we come to the steps leading above ground. Da Nang is there to help us out. When he emerges, the face of the man behind me has flushed a deep red. His chest heaves, though he tries to appear calm. 'Tunnel is a bit small,' is all he says. At that moment I envy his powers of denial. But I haven't accounted for M and her refusal to deny.

'This place is haunted,' she says calmly, examining the grit on her hands. 'I saw people from another time.'

We are in the sunlight. A breeze blows through the rubber trees, but the breath of the tunnel is inside us. I ask Da Nang if there have been instances of people panicking, seeing things, scrambling to get out.

'Every time. There's always someone who sees the past. Those who can't see think the ones who can are crazy. We know these tunnels are crowded. There isn't enough room for all of us who died.'

The rest of the group joins us and the change begins in Da Nang's speech. I notice that when she speaks privately her English is fluent, but when she speaks to the group it is pidgin, exaggerated for effect.

'After all, tunnel is designed for slender people who not eat much, because there not enough food. In tunnel, you eat anything, mouse, dog, cat.'

We follow her to an outdoor area of square concrete tables set into the earth. Concrete benches for seating. The young German asks if they'd really eaten cats and dogs and mice in the tunnels.

'Of course we did,' says Da Nang. 'In the forest, to survive we eat anything, whatever we catch. Some tourists have try mouse and snake also. They say most delicious is mouse, have you try?'

'No,' says the German, 'I think I will forgo that experience.'

'How about dog and cat? You don't want try?'

'I reserve the right to say no to certain experiences. You don't have to try everything.'

'If you say.'

'I tried goat once,' says the man brightly.

'Okay! I apologize, no mouse today on menu. Only roasted cassava.'

'Cassava. Is it like tapioca?'

'Same thing. A staple for tunnel-dwellers because of nutritional properties and it so easy to prepare.'

I am oddly gratified that the only people who try the cassava – a root vegetable, by no means an exotic dish – are M, the young Asian in the sweats and myself. Amongst us, an air of conspiracy as we help ourselves to the smoky, fibrous tuber that tastes of the tunnels and gives us a quick sense of what it is like to live underground and eat a single meal a day. To wash it down, there is muddy herbal tea the colour of the Mekong Delta. No one else, not even the German who has tasted goat (once), will try the modest, filling repast.

From where we sit, I can see the entrance to the tunnels. I know what lies in those narrow corridors, the crowds of men and women and children crawling for food, carrying the wounded to makeshift stations where they will be tended to and healed, if healing is possible, the crippled on narrow pallets measured to fit, the man or woman in front scrambling backwards, or squatting; and the first level below ground, and the one below that, how deep it extends, the secondary routes to the top, the passages that branch off from each of the platforms to the rooms used for storage or convalescence or prayer, the engineered vision of the labyrinth that stretches for miles in every direction; and there in the sunshine, the taste of cassava lingering on my senses, I'm certain that those who had lived and died underground are still there, peaceably waiting, avoiding certain corridors at certain times of day so they won't meet the visitors who come to share for a moment their eternal spaces, moving upwards or downwards or sideways, a vast silent gathering that fills the square or rectangular or tubular spaces with mild electricity; and even as we get up and gather our things and take the van back to District One, an idea seems to come to me all at once, that everywhere around us are those who have been buried alive by the war, who wish to emerge from the dark into the noise of the day, who watch us with longing.

I take the photograph from my notebook and show it to Da Nang. She gazes for a long moment at the young woman on the motorcycle, then her slender hands reach to touch the hands of the woman and it is clear that she is speechless and speechlessness is not a condition to which she is accustomed. She tells us she has never seen a picture of her grandmother as a young woman, though she has often tried to imagine what kind of young woman she might have been. To her it seems a miracle that the picture she is now holding had been taken by my father. By the time the van drops us at our hotel, it is decided that we will rent a car to take us from Saigon to Hanoi, and Da Nang will accompany us as our guide.

That night, I remark how strange it is that we saw the same hallucination in the tunnels of Cu Chi. 'It wasn't a hallucination and it wasn't strange at all,' says M. 'When you sleep with someone, your heads close or touching, then it happens that you share dreams. Visions travel from one head and arrive in the other, it's only natural.'

I TRY NOT TO THINK about it but there it is, March 30. Soon it will be All Fool's Day.

Da Nang and Michael, the agency's driver, pick us up from the hotel at a quarter to eight. We travel Highway One up to Highway Twenty. On both sides of the road are coffee plantations, churches and cemeteries, testimony to the French colonists who brought Catholicism and coffee to Vietnam. The cemeteries extend for miles. It is all we see for the first few hours out of Saigon. Among the graves are those Da Nang describes as local. Vietnamese who'd been converted to Catholicism by the French.

'You call it cemetery, we call it quiet city,' says Da Nang from the front seat.

'Because the dead don't speak?'

'Yeah, walk, no talk.'

There is nothing quiet about the architecture of the quiet cities. If anything, they shout wealth and extravagance. Towers two or three storeys high, of glazed tiles and ceramic figurines. Mausoleums that include functioning bedrooms, kitchens and baths. Tombs that resemble elegant homes and mansions. Elaborate Hindu temples with Sanskrit markings. Pagodas with intricate gold flourishes. Feathered columns of dragons and mythical fish and fantastical creatures never seen. But hours of watching decorative death monuments begin to weigh on me, and when the landscape changes it is a relief. A village of stilt houses, canoes tethered to the pilings: the dwellings of the Cambodian boat people who came to Vietnam to escape Pol Pot. Built over a lagoon several metres deep and filled with fish farms, crab traps and rice paddies, houses that are self-maintained ecologies, easy to dismantle if a quick move were needed. We watch the floating village give way to a sea of pink that extends far into the distance, carpets of delicate flowers held aloft on glossy leaves rising high off the water.

'It's the season of the water hyacinth,' Da Nang says. But the mention of hyacinths is not enough to dispel the silence that has settled upon us.

'Death, death, death,' says M.

'What?'

'Always talking about death.'

'Not always.'

'Most of the time.'

'It's true,' says Da Nang. 'But you can't blame me.'

'Yes, I can. Why can't I?'

'We've seen too much of it.'

The sun is setting as we pull into the hill town of Dalat. A band of bright pink stretches away to the south. The sky has cleared and the air is cool, smelling of pine and mown grass. At the hotel, Da Nang says goodnight and leaves without explanation. We have dinner at the restaurant and walk up the hill road, but the climb is steep and soon we go back to the room. We are to meet our guide at 10.30 the following morning to make it to Qui Nhon on the coast by nightfall. 'Too late,' Da Nang had said, '10.30 too late,' and when we come down at ten, she is waiting in the lobby, not pleased that we are yet to have breakfast.

I ask where she's spent the night.

'Dalat full of hotel,' she says in the car. 'At your hotel, only basement room available. I didn't want to stay in the basement. I'm not a prisoner.'

'And Michael?'

'He sleeps in car,' she says shortly. At the wheel, silent Michael nods and shifts to second gear for the climb.

Mid-morning, we stop at a clifftop shack with broad views of the valley and plains below, a family-run restaurant, just opened for the day. The waitress, middle-aged and muscular, has a child anchored to her hip. Montagnard was the name given to the mountain people by the French. One among the thousands displaced by government decree, it's unlikely she thinks of herself as Montagnard. The republic took control of all land with a high agricultural yield, which included homes built on the fertile coffee-growing highlands. They'd been cut off from the mainland and treated as if they weren't really Vietnamese, cut off for generations until they began to believe it. They made mistakes, but then they weren't politicians. They befriended the colonials, the French and the Americans, which damned them forever in the eyes of their countrymen. When Saigon fell and the North Vietnamese moved into the south, they forced the mountain people off the mountains, executed some, put others in prison, restricted them in every way. It was revenge for a crime they didn't know they'd committed. Large numbers of Montagnard fled to Cambodia and Thailand. Many were left stranded, treated as tribal usurpers, traitors who pretended to be Vietnamese but thought of themselves as whole and separate. The largest group of Montagnard outside Vietnam is in Greensboro, North Carolina.

'They were on the wrong side of the war,' Da Nang says, 'losing side. They tried to protest, but the government does not enjoy protest and they were persuaded to give up.' She puts down her coffee cup and makes a cutting motion with her hand.

To know history is to know loss, and the displaced know it best. I feel some growing sympathy for the taciturn woman with the child on her hip. On the wall is a framed picture torn from a magazine of a snow-covered mountain. The plastic flowers at the table haven't been dusted in weeks. I notice a pile of rubber slippers and sandals at the entrance, as well as a pair of spit-shined leather shoes. I ask the woman, with Da Nang translating, if we should leave our shoes outside.

'No need. Sometimes we also forget.'

She nods at a boy of four running between the tables, bent on mayhem, a pair of muddy yellow Crocs on his feet.

'How big is your family?'

'Five of us and one more on the way,' she says, patting her belly.

'All of you live here?'

She nods at a curtained-off section behind the cash counter.

'It must be crowded.'

'My daughter is leaving soon. She is marrying Vietnamese.'

But her manner changes, as if she knows she has made a mistake by saying *Vietnamese*. She looks at my notebook and pen.

'Are you from the press?'

'No, I'm writing a ghost story.'

Da Nang's translation of the last phrase is too long for my simple explanation, which I hoped would make the woman smile. But she clears away the cups and doesn't return from the kitchen. In the car, I ask Da Nang what she said. 'I tell her you writer,' she says in the pidgin she uses when she is annoyed. 'I tell her I don't know what kind of writer you are.' To change the subject, she points at a bike that has fallen over the side of the road into a ditch. A group of schoolchildren stand around it.

'Oh,' she says, 'accident. Did you know twenty-two to twenty-five people die on the roads every day, more people than American War?'

She gestures at the crashed bike and laughs mirthlessly. 'Driver is foreigner, bike go down three metres. Look at the kids walking to school. Long walk!' She thinks for a moment and adds: 'In the sun!'

As we pass them, the schoolchildren turn to us and I see the face of a child I saw in the tunnels of Cu Chi. One among the lost on the great ladder leading nowhere. To see her now in the daylight is baffling, but only for a moment.

My mind is tuned to ghosts.

We are speeding on a downhill road of curves and switchbacks and SLOW signs. Michael's style is to accelerate into blind turns, overtake two-wheelers and tailgate other cars. When he passes a vehicle, he touches the ripe pimple on his chin.

'Is he drunk,' M whispers, 'or does he just not care?'

I glance at the rear-view mirror, but Michael's eyes are hidden behind black wraparounds. Ahead of us, a new road is being cut into the mountains. For long sections, I can see our route all the way to the plains, interrupted here and there by looping U-turns. We slow behind a funeral convoy, two cars and a van flanked by motorcycles. Wisps of paper money fly out of the van's back window. Two boys on a motorcycle keep pace. The pillion-rider holds a torch in each hand, black smoke billowing into the late afternoon sunshine. Part of a new trend, city families burying their dead in the countryside where there is no shortage of space. Government posters say: *Burn Don't Bury*. The dead end up in an urn in the shrine in a small apartment. If the family can afford it, they buy a plot somewhere in the open.

The cortège turns off into a tree-lined lane. Once free of the funeral, Michael opens up at his pleasure and in two hours we rejoin Highway One. We are well on our way to the coast.

At two the next morning I'm brought awake, not knowing what woke me. Then I remember. Taking into account the Delhi–Qui Nhon time difference, at that exact moment eleven years earlier, my wife had stepped into gravity's oblivion and left a one-line note: *Nobody is to blame*. Ever since, I've wondered, who was Nobody? Was it me? As it does each year, my body remembers. I climb out of bed and sit in the armchair in the dark, air-conditioning cold on my skin, no sense of time having passed since that night in Delhi. I stay in the chair until M sits up and puts on her glasses.

'I was so worried. I woke up three times and you weren't there.'

Hours pass in a state of trance or communion. I want to sleep, but towards dawn I hear, I swear, a new sound in the quiet room. The nearness and strangeness of it wakes me fully and then it comes again. A series of soft thuds, a brief pause, more thuds. I know it is a gentle knocking against the wall by the bed. At erratic intervals the knocking resumes, soft and unsure, always on my side of the room. There's a way of putting a stop to it, I'll introduce my dead wife to M. But just as the solution occurs to me, the knocking stops and perky Vietnamese pop starts to play in the garden below. It is six in the morning. The breakfast buffet has begun.

In an hour, we are on the two-hundred-and-fifty-mile stretch to Huế. We pass a hamlet on a hill and a dozen sandstone towers like the temples of Cambodia and India. Not tall or imposing, but built for utilitarian purposes, set at intervals among humble flat-roofed houses. It could be Bihar or the Central Provinces of India. I ask Da Nang if the houses and temples were built by the Chams. She says a few hundred worship at the temples, dismissing them as an agricultural people of no interest. Then, brightening, she says, only six hundred and fifty miles to Hanoi. In response, Michael's foot falls heavy to the accelerator. Her dismissal is an official attitude. Vietnam's minorities have to constantly prove themselves worthy. They make up more than fifty ethnic groups including the Indianized Chams, as unwelcome in Vietnam as the Montagnard, for similar reasons. Unlike Indian nationalism which comes and goes in waves and for long periods existed only in pockets, Vietnamese nationalism has never waned. A thousand years of Chinese rule created the nationalist idea. Anti-Chinese fervour has only grown with time and goes much deeper than the more recent distaste for Americans. Da Nang is an embodiment of Vietnamese resentments, old and new.

We stop at an eatery where she orders white rice, sweet pork, water spinach cooked with garlic, light omelettes, cucumber soup. The cucumbers are sliced so thin, says Da Nang to the proprietress, that the slices may cut her tongue. It is her usual way of joking and, as usual, nobody laughs. Throughout the meal I hear the screaming of pigs being slaughtered behind the bamboo wall of the eatery, and I can't bring myself to try the pork. Then we are back on the winding mountain road and the mist clears to sudden sunshine.

We pass Da Nang (the town), but don't stop.

'Nothing to see,' says our guide, 'soon we'll be at Hai Van, Sea of Clouds, longest tunnel in all of Southeast Asia. Six and a half kilometres!'

I've been dreading it all day. Cu Chi has taught me to acknowledge the tethered spirits who call enclosed spaces home. And before the ordeal of the tunnel, the ordeal of a new freeway and its 75 mph speed limit. Michael sighs with pleasure as he changes gears to top cruising speed. Built high over dense tree cover to stay clear of monsoon overflows, the freeway overlooks the tops of tall pines. There are no villages or people almost for an hour and only one other car on three lanes of road. Locals prefer to bypass the freeway because the toll is too high.

'You can imagine,' says Da Nang, 'one hundred thousand per trip is a lot of ding-dong.'

But the tunnel is clean and well lit. Ventilation ducts and emergency call services every few metres. South of Huế, we find the tunnels of the demilitarized zone, different from the tunnels of Cu Chi, with high ceilings and wood beams. You can stroll and stop and shop. Entire families have lived and worked there. The Vietnamese take pride in their tunnels, the inspired constructions of Cu Chi and the DMZ. But economic power flexes in unexpected ways, and now the pride is misdirected. It is the Koreans and Japanese who make the new tunnels of Vietnam, through the mountains, at great cost and little saving of time.

Once we are off the desolate freeway where no vehicles are to be seen, after the long run through the tunnel, we enter the arterial street named Nguyen That Than, Ho Chi Minh's birth name. Nguyen is the name of an old dynasty. As an image-conscious young revolutionary Ho didn't want to be associated with royalty or the elite.

'Uncle Ho,' says Da Nang. 'Like Uncle Sam, but better.'

As a teenager, Da Nang's stoic nature was captivated by the story of Ho Chi Minh's three decades of exile, when he travelled the world organizing resistance to French rule, sometimes working as a military strategist, sometimes as an intelligence agent, using false passports and more than a hundred pseudonyms, holding all kinds of odd jobs, kitchen helper on merchant ships, baker in New York City, dishwasher in West Ealing, pastry chef at under-the-radar restaurants, gardener, oven stoker, sweeper, photo retoucher. As she grew older and learned to abhor China's incursions into Vietnam, Da Nang successfully forgot the inconvenient details of Ho's story. That at the age of thirty-six, in a Canton restaurant, he married a twenty-one-year-old Chinese midwife named Zeng Xueming, who would deliver thousands of children and never one of her own. Ho fled the country six months later, half a step ahead of Chiang Kai-Shek's anti-communist purge, but in those six months, to Ho's joy, Zeng fell pregnant with their child, a child she was convinced to abort by her mother who was wary of Ho's precarious status in the country, rightly as it turned out. Abandoned but never forgotten, Zeng didn't marry again and lived to the age of eighty-six. For years afterwards, Ho yearned for his bride with lips like petals, hair fragrant as moss in the rain. In his wanderings, he wrote her letters of undisguised love intercepted without his knowledge by senior members of his own party. She was inconvenient to the cult of personality they were building around him. It was inconvenient that she was Chinese. Inconvenient she was Catholic, like their French oppressors. Most inconvenient, she was not interested in politics. None of these things mattered to her husband who was blinded by her beauty. Da Nang also chose to forget that, during his years as a sailor, Ho had a girlfriend in every port. Women were attracted to his visionary articles and speeches, his dreamy eyes and sensuous mouth. A municipal worker in Paris suggested she bear him a child to further his dream of an independent Vietnam. A seamstress in Vladivostok said he should stop wearing Western clothes and dress like the nationalist hero he was sure to become. This he did, suits and ties set aside for khaki jackets and guerrilla pyjamas, his clean-cut look replaced with a long chin beard and Zapata moustache. There was the Anglo-Indian schoolteacher who quoted Keats and Marx, sometimes in the same breath, who translated Ho's poems with rare acuity, and thrilled to hear the new slogan shouted on the streets of Calcutta: *Amar Nam, Tomar Nam, Vietnam*. And there was Nguyen Minh Khai, deputed to Hong Kong from Trung Ky as his secretary, while he worked at the Orient Bureau of the Comintern and called himself Nguyen Ai Quoc, Nguyen the Patriot. He requested permission to marry her although he was still married to Zeng. The ceremony never took place. Minh was detained by the British and executed by a French firing squad. Da Nang's curated forgetfulness about Ho Chi Minh's past coincided nicely with the party's aim to reinvent him as the celibate father figure, Uncle Ho. He didn't live to see the unified Vietnam, but he was no tormented soul broken by the glacial tide of history. He knew it was a matter of time. When he lay in his final illness and faces from his past swam out of the dark, Zeng's was radiant with happiness. Ho whispered out of earshot of his caretakers, in a voice soft as rain, 'I will read my letters to you soon, my wife, each word will tell you I've been constant, even if I haven't been faithful. I wait for you as I have waited these decades and will wait across the great divide that stretches between the living and the dead, my love a beacon to guide you back to me.'

In time, a hypnotized people came to revere Uncle Ho as Saint Ho. During his unsainted years, when he was still on the verge of beatitude, he went to India. My father was disappointed not to have met him then. In Hanoi, four years after Ho's death, when he was still the guiding light of the long struggle for Vietnamese wholeness, a copy of Ho Chi Minh's testament was presented to George as a memento.

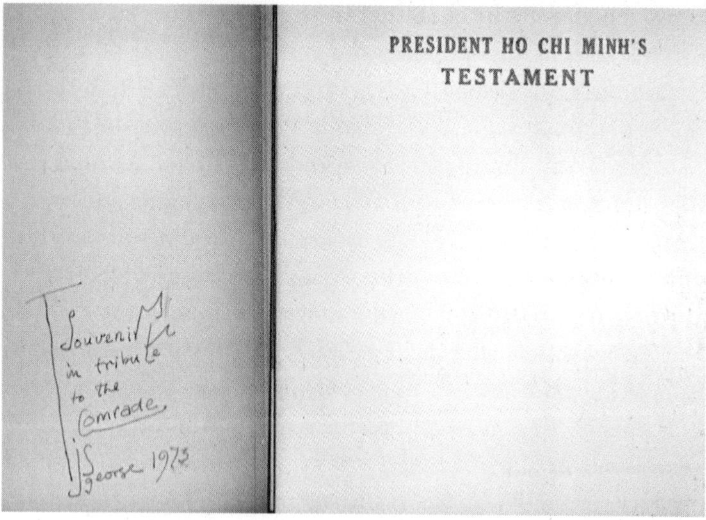

The street named after the beloved revolutionary stretches into the distance, but the young have deserted the district in droves, leaving their parents and grandparents in charge of family homes now fallen into ruin. No businesses to be seen, just the occasional shop or eatery. The weather too has turned against them. The old ones don't remember a time when typhoons and floods were so frequent or when the humidity stayed all year long. Unsurprisingly, Da Nang has a nationalistic take on typhoons:

'Filipinos are our neighbours. They always send their typhoons to us. But we are good neighbours. We take the typhoons and protect Laos.'

Our night stop is near Huế's moated, two-hundred-year-old citadel, now a tourist hub, the bombing it endured in the Tet Offensive forgotten by the hustlers and touts who petition backpackers at all times of day. The police too are champions of the new. At every junction on the great street named after Uncle Ho, traffic policemen pull over truckers to check weights, loads and papers, and the truckers hand over envelopes. The police, on one-hour shifts, work diligently. The team including the supervisor at the office will share in the spoils. But Da Nang won't tolerate criticism of her country, even if, in the interests of fairness, I offer criticism of mine.

'India has just become the number one country on the corruption index, most corrupt in the world,' I say.

'Yes, you must have learn from China,' says Da Nang.

'Vietnam is number two.'

'We must have learn from you,' she says, ominously smiling.

'Must have learned from somebody.'

'Here we no say corrupt, we say envelope. It sound more educated.'

'More cultured.'

'In Vietnam, drug dealers get automatic death penalty,' says Da Nang boastfully. 'In jail we have to feed them rice, keep them clothed. Too much expense! But drug users not executed. They sent to re-education camps.'

'By re-education you mean tortured in prison?'

'We prefer to say re-education, sound more educated.'

'More cultured.'

'Exactly.'

When we stop for lunch, she asks the price of the meal as she usually does. For shrimp, mackerel and rice, the proprietress wants two hundred thousand dong, price adjusted for foreigners.

'Two hundred thousand?' says Da Nang incredulously.

'Go,' says the woman, 'don't eat here.'

Da Nang's reply rings like a curse: 'You'll never be rich.'

I am happy to go elsewhere. Two tour buses full of passengers have arrived and the drivers are yelling directions into portable microphones. The passengers shout too. The smell of urine from the busy toilets is overpowering. Women squat near the buses and wash with bottles of water. But Da Nang, still smarting from the exchange with the proprietress, prefers to deflect to the traditional enemy.

'You think these people loud? Chinese three times louder! They stay in hotel, in one year destroy everything. Europeans stay in hotel, take five years to destroy everything. Chinese don't like to spend. Always looking for cheaper, cheapest, saying, no, no, too much ding-dong! I take tour group to other country, sometimes foreigners say, *ni hao, ni hao*. So, I put Vietnam flag on bus. Then when they say *ni hao*, I say, no, not Chinese, we are Vietnamese. You know, Vietnam?' She makes a machine-gun motion with her hands. 'Bang, bang, bang!'

But something has occurred to her.

She says to M, 'You not Chinese, right?'

'Only half,' says M.

'Then we only half enemy,' says Da Nang.

At the next restaurant, we take our seats with a new camaraderie, Da Nang's indignation on our behalf has changed something. The bill would have been ours to pay, but her anger at the restaurant owner was genuine, and I was touched. Over coffee, I ask, at last, about her grandmother. 'My father died in September 1967,' she says. 'I was born in June 1968. My mom got a pension, but no work was available because Vietnam was embargoed. She left me with my grandmother. My grandma cannot look after a naughty girl, so she threw me to the nuns. At that time, my name was Coi, which means orphan. My grandma gave me the name because when I was born I had no father and later I had no mother. But I didn't want to be Coi. I named myself after my father's home town. When I turned twenty-three, I was sent to some nuns in the Philippines as a refugee. I told them, I can't stay here, I have no relatives, no friends, how can I survive? The nuns told me, don't worry, you can be the cook. I stayed for four years. I learned to cook pho and bun, what needs more time to cook, what needs less. I enjoy my cooking because you always enjoy your own flavours. I became restaurant manager. Then my grandma started the agency and called me to work in Saigon. Now she also calls me Da Nang. Unless she's angry. Then she says, hey, Coi.'

PASSING THIS WAY THIRTY YEARS EARLIER, my father observed that southerners were darker. 'We also smile more,' a woman in Saigon told him. A port worker in the north-eastern city of Haiphong explained that the south could afford to be friendly. There were no typhoons and no winter, the soil was fertile, the forests thick. Northerners had a difficult life. Where was the time to smile?

On the fifth day, a hundred kilometres from Hanoi, the difference between south and north is apparent still. No emergency call numbers by the side of the road. No safety railings on the national highway. Cattle and dogs and pedestrians cross at will. No women to be seen. Only men service the tollbooths. The countryside changes to paddy fields and roadside restaurants similar to the makeshift dhabas of Delhi. No spas, no café sua da, no neon, no signs offering massages, fewer advertisements, no pencil skirts or suits on scooters, no sunglasses. The landscape settles into character. Men urinate by the side of the highway. Road discipline is replaced by frenzy and dust, Saigon's shiny finish long gone. As we near Hanoi, I look over the passages I've copied from my father's notes of 1973. His description of aftermath is more recognizable here than it was in the south:

> *When you saw a concentration of bomb craters on both sides of the road, you knew there was a bridge ahead. Often it was no more than a culvert of a few feet. Not one link was left unbombed. The further you went, the more terrible the depredations. At the end of this 600 km trip, I was left with undying admiration for the sturdiness of Soviet jeeps, and my stomach muscles, and for Nguyen Phuc Chau and her people. When we reached Vinh Linh the drivers got heroes' welcome with kisses and embraces. The real luxury at end of trip was the cold water well bath. You were a man again.*

After driving more than three hundred kilometres a day, 1,735 kilometres over five days and four nights, we arrive in Nguyen Phuc Chau's city.

We circle the chaos of flyovers and hit the first traffic jam of the journey. Cars and trucks weave in and out of wavering, shifting lanes. Ambulances are stuck like everyone else, sirens blaring. Drivers honk for no reason. We navigate hundreds of two-wheelers whose riders speak on cell phones or text. Where we've covered fifty kilometres in an hour on the highway, it takes an hour to crawl eight kilometres to our Airbnb.

On the Street of Bamboo Lattices, where no bamboo or lattices are to be seen, we find the entrance to our home for the next five days. A wet alley between a shop selling SIM cards and one selling clothes, the tiny opening blocked by a congee vendor and her elderly customers. To the left, a doorway where two medium-sized rats scamper up a staircase. All along the wall, clothes hung to dry form puddles at my feet. A woman stands at a door and guards a room. At the end of the winding alley, a flight of stairs painted lime green. Above this, two more flights and a newly made tin staircase that shakes with each step. At the top, a black door with an electronic lock. The lock and door are modern additions to the tenement. I go back to the car to get M, and we pass the rats, the stinking alley, the woman in the doorway, and take the wobbly staircase to the black door. She checks her phone and punches in the code, and we find two rooms, brick walls, a bed with clean white sheets, a corridor converted into a shower, cooking utensils on a pull-away counter and, inches above us, a tin roof. The air is thick with dust and the heat of the day.

'What do you think?' I ask.

'I don't know,' says M.

She won't look at me.

'We can't stay here.'

'Okay.'

She covers her face with her hands and weeps, freely and silently.

'I found us a bad place.'

We go back to the car and Da Nang takes charge. 'It's impossible,' she says. She calls the man from whom we've booked the place, who suggests we leave our suitcases at a shop on the street and take what we need for the night and go to the room. We ask if we can pay for a day and get a refund on the rest. He is outraged but the outrage is false. He's done the same to other travellers. We give it up and drive to a hotel in the tourist district. Da Nang checks us in and leaves, promising to set up a meeting with her grandmother. In the room, we unpack and think of a bath and dinner. We sit on the bed and take off our shoes. We lean against the pillows and are asleep. It is nine in the evening.

The phone wakes us early. Da Nang has booked a morning flight back to Saigon. Can we come to Cong Café in half an hour? We pick up four takeaway coffees from the hotel restaurant and walk to the end of the street. The café has not yet opened. At a table outside sits Nguyen Phuc Chau. She wears a teal ao dai and wide-legged pyjamas and she is frowning at something Da Nang has said. When I hold out my hand, she surprises me by folding hers in a namaste. I show her the picture George had taken forty-five years earlier. She barely glances at it. She is more interested in a photograph of him as a college student, around the time of Indian independence, twenty-five years before their first meeting.

'Yes,' she says. 'Handsome man.'

Her English is perfect and unaccented.

'Why did you never tell me about him?' Da Nang asks.

'Because I don't like to talk about myself in the past, makes me sad,' the old woman says.

'Why didn't you marry him?' her granddaughter asks.

'He was already married,' Nguyen Phuc Chau replies, glancing shyly at me. 'But when he was teaching here in 1986, I know he thought about staying.' And as if continuing an old conversation, she says, 'I'm sorry I gave you to the nuns. My husband was a soldier. Those were different times. We felt we didn't deserve family or happiness when so many had died. It's why I moved back to the north.'

'When I was with the nuns, I thought you hated me.'

'No, I did not hate you,' the old woman says. 'I was afraid of you.'

'Afraid of a child?' says Da Nang.

Her grandmother blinks once or twice and is silent.

'You were afraid because your daughter had left you and gone,' says M, all of a sudden. 'You didn't want to be attached to anyone.'

Without warning, tears fall from the old woman's eyes.

'Only after I started the travel agency, only then,' she says. 'Then I knew I could hold on to you.'

We stay for some time, sipping our coffee as, slowly, the street comes alive. When we get up to leave, I ask if I can take a photograph.

'Please, no,' says Nguyen Phuc Chau, 'I want him to remember me on the motorcycle, when I was free and young.'

INDEPENDENCE

THUMPAMON, 1943 | BOMBAY, 1947 | BIHAR, 1965 | HONG KONG, 1967

'Keep moving if you want to stay alive.'

'Isn't that what they say about sharks?'

'Sharks and us.'

OF FIVE SONS, FOUR ARE FOOTBALL players, bodybuilders, military history enthusiasts, small-time businessmen. In short, outgoing young hooligans. The middle son is freakishly quiet. When he begins to do well at school, he's put on a special diet. His father says it's a way to *train the brain*. A cup of lukewarm Horlicks before sleeping, and on waking a tablespoon of cod liver oil which rises biliously in his throat for hours afterwards. Worse are the head massages administered by the old cook on Sunday afternoons, an ordeal to be endured without complaint as the man's heavy hands drum on his scalp.

'See?' says Baby, the oldest, in the booming voice that appears when his father is not near. 'Better not to have a brain to train.'

There is a sister, and only she rates a real name. Saro. The boys are given generic labels made up on the spot. The oldest had been a baby once. But to be called Uncle Baby in old age by young nephews and nieces? A torment. The second oldest is Small Son. The middle boy is Son or Sonny (his brothers call him Brain Boy). And the youngest are Little Son and Young Son.

Thumpamon has no school, only a collection of dirt streets and a church square. This is the centre around which all things grow, the priests' spacious quarters, scattered farmhouses, a graveyard, a general store, a bank run by the same family that owns the store. The brothers walk thirty-five minutes each way to attend Gregorios Memorial School near Pathanamthitta. The walk is an opportunity for hilarity.

'Brain Boy, are you enjoying the cod liver yet?'

'Does it help your brain when cook drums on it like a tabla?'

'How much Shakespeare have you by-hearted so far, donkey?'

To dissuade him from studying English literature, rather than useful subjects such as law or medicine, his father summons Son into the long front room. This is where important occasions are marked. Marriages and engagements. Priests' visits. Special prayers. Illnesses and funeral rites. The house is a modest four-room structure that stands on a small plot with a freshwater well. His father, the district magistrate, takes some pride in the modesty of his home – it's a way of letting the village know that he won't be bribed. He is a man of *moral fibre*, a phrase he likes to use with his children.

The talk takes place on the boy's fifteenth birthday.

'I have a question regarding your literature textbook,' the magistrate says in English. (With his mother, Son speaks only Malayalam.) 'What is a daffodil?'

'A flower.'

'Have you seen this flower?'

'I have not, yet I know it exists. Like God.'

'Leave God out of it. What is a robin redbreast?'

'A small bird with a red face and beard. What else could it be?'

'I'm asking a serious question with a serious purpose. Don't be acting like a big man.'

'Sorry, Appa.'

'Sorry, what?'

'I'm sorry, Magistrate Jacob.'

'I accept your apology, boy. Now, what is autumn?'

'Season of mellow mists and fruitfulness,' says Son, in the rousing elocution voice that has won him school competitions.

'Have you ever experienced such a season?'

'I have not, Magistrate Jacob.'

'And yet you memorized a poem that describes it. Good. This is my last question, and depending on your answer you may study what you like. If it is wrong, you will study law, medicine or engineering.'

'Answer now?'

'Of course, now. Question: of what use is it to learn by heart pretty words about birds, flowers and seasons that do not exist in our world?'

The magistrate gestures at the fields beyond the veranda. At the trees covered in dust. At a herd of black buffaloes that sways past in the lane outside. Son's eyes follow the sweep of his father's hand and he watches the big-boned animals disappear into the late afternoon light. He doesn't reply immediately, having learned the uses of silence. His father settles into the cane easy chair with the long leg-rests and waits. The boy shifts from foot to foot. No one speaks until the evening's shadows begin to fall upon the gravel by the veranda.

'It shows me there's a world beyond our poor village,' Son says, his grey eyes on the high mud wall that faces the house. 'Even if I never experience it for myself, knowing it is there will make me a better man.'

The magistrate fixes his son with a suspicious stare and is about to say something when there's a shout from the kitchen. His wife, calling the family for the evening meal. He rises, adjusts his at-home lungi and collects his eyeglasses and walking stick. The shadow leaves his face. Father and son go in to eat as if a contract has been settled.

Sent to the then-distant metropolis of Madras in the neighbouring state of Tamil Nadu, he becomes aware of other distances, the history being enacted outside his ken, to the north of the country. He begins to use another of his three given names, a new name for a new life, George rather than Jacob. In a few weeks, Thumpamon seems remote, as far away as boyhood. Mixed with excitement, there is melancholy. He fills the emptiness with walks around the campus. In a leafy, never-before-visited part of the grounds, he finds a one-storey tile-roofed house. Inside is silence and solitude: a library. He can borrow whatever books he wants, return them and borrow others. One writer leads to the next. The pleasure lies in accident and improvisation, but the library limits his wandering to the classics.

He acts in plays put up by the theatrical group. He directs a comedy. He buys a suit. With an Honours in English from the Madras Christian College, he takes a second journey – longer than the first: two nights and three days by train and bus – to Bombay, where he moves into his oldest brother's rented apartment in the middle-class suburb of Mahim. The apartment has two rooms. Baby, his wife and two children sleep in the small inner bedroom. George uses the living room. The front door opens to the street. The washroom is shared with the neighbours.

In his first weeks of wandering about the city, he keeps returning to the ocean. It is everywhere. Visible from the main promenades and hidden behind railway stations, cul-de-sacs and dead ends. Choppy swells stretch to the near horizon, so different from the placid backwaters of his home state. The ocean puts salt in the air at all times and he comes to rely on its tang. Metal rusts quickly in the salt. New buildings acquire a weather-beaten stain, as if they've been battered for years.

Sometimes, he stops at Paradise Café for strong sugary milk tea served with a flaky khari biscuit. The waiter is a wiry old Parsi in a sudreh who bangs glasses of water and tea on the chipped marble tabletop. Like the other patrons, George drinks first the water, then the tea. On the wall, portraits of Zarathustra, Queen Elizabeth and Gandhi share space with a Coca-Cola advertisement. He pays with coins. Leaving Paradise, he finds sand on the sidewalk and steps out of his shoes to feel the grit against his feet. The sensation brings a smile to his face. The Parsi waiter comes out to smoke a Capstan.

'I did the same thing,' the old man says, 'when I first came here. Enjoy. Only thing free in this city.'

His brothers advise him to try for a government job, but no one knows how to go about it. He sends job applications to the air force and to newspapers. Handwritten on a sheet of paper and delivered in person. An offer arrives from the only organization that cares to reply, *The Free Press Journal*. The editor, Sadanand, is known to hire anyone who asks for a job, but most new hires are sacked in a fortnight. George is put on the news desk as a subeditor. He is nineteen. In the lonely hours of the night shift, between seven in the evening and two or three in the morning, the day's headlines and top stories are decided. The glamour of the life comes to him then, and something more. To be a journalist is to be a figure of nobility. Now, at last, he feels touched by luck – to have landed in this profession in 1947, during the critical months after Independence, while the nation builds itself one brick at a time.

He becomes close to Sadanand, who seems to live at the office, thriving on a diet of black tea and peppery South Indian food. His eccentric work habits ensure the paper misses no stories, in particular the seemingly insignificant tales of calamity among ordinary people.

'Do you know what they want, *Free Press* readers?'

'Upliftment and reassurance?'

'Bosh,' says Sadanand. 'They want heartbreak, not happy stories. Go write something that will break the heart and enrage the mind!'

If that's what he wants, George will go more than one better. At his desk, he finds a clean sheet of paper and draws a square. He divides the square into four parts and writes a word in each, *Heartbreakers, Tearjerkers, Muckrakers, Rage-makers*. For the first instalment in his new system, he goes to Paradise Café and speaks to the waiter and files a story headlined 'The Sea at his Feet'. In his private filing system, he puts it under Tearjerker.

In a year, he is promoted to assistant editor.

OVER THE COURSE OF HIS WRITING LIFE, George writes twenty books of politics, biography, reference and journalism, of which sixteen are in English and four in Malayalam. During India's independence movement, newspaper work is a patriotic calling rather than a profession. It makes him the kind of writer who can't start a sentence with the first-person pronoun. The exception is *Four Months on a Cargo Ship*, written in a high Malayalam difficult to follow if you're unschooled in the language. Published in 1960 when he is thirty-two, he uses the first-person without self-consciousness. Although he makes his living writing in English, the imaginative leaps, the digressions into unexpected, contingent areas, the delight in play, all of this occurs only in Malayalam.

Four Months on a Cargo Ship is the account of his time as a cook on the SS *Jalakanya* (Sea Maiden), which plies between Bombay, Hamburg, Bremen, London and Newcastle. Still working with the *Free Press*, he convinces Sadanand to let him go by promising regular reports from the cities where the ship will dock. In a chapter titled 'Sea Duties', he describes an interview near the headquarters of the Bombay Port Trust.

For a few hours in the afternoon, once the office rush is over, it's easy to get a seat on the second-class local from Mahim to Colaba. The train compartment bakes in the sun but the hot breeze is a blessing, even if it's mixed with the soot and grit pumped by the engine. He has had a cold-water bucket bath before he left, and now, twenty minutes into the journey, shirt sticking to his back, he's ready for another. The train stops at Dadar where the vegetable vendors enter the compartment. He moves his feet to make room for the baskets. Smells of coriander and mint fill the air. Then come the fisherwomen with dripping baskets of fresh prawn and Bombay Duck, and in minutes the compartment is as redolent as Sassoon Dock. Reluctantly, for it's been pleasant to sit by the window and let the breeze play over him, he leaves the train at Churchgate and takes a bus to Ballard Estate. As he walks to the navy station, the city grows quieter. The cafés, restaurants, cinemas and stores become smaller and fewer in number. The walls are higher, more impenetrable, and beyond them he sees the masts of schooners and the funnels of steamships. At the merchant navy interviewing room, he applies for the post of 'messing supervisor'. His job, says the interviewing officer, requires no qualifications or previous experience. It was created to suit the trade union. 'Your work is to stay quiet and do nothing,' the officer says. 'You can get up late, say around eight-thirty, in time for breakfast. After breakfast, a good sleep is in order and then we'll call you for lunch. Afterwards, a nap before we wake you for dinner. After dinner, follow the old rule: early to bed.' The man is joking, but only partly. George does no actual supervising or cooking. His cabin is below decks in the cooks' quarters. When the officers understand he is a journalist, he's welcome topside.

In 1953, he visits London for the first time. 'It was the greatest thing you could do in those days,' George tells me. 'To see London. The street names and parks and buildings were familiar from books I'd read, as familiar as the name of my home town in Kerala, or the mill district near the *Free Press* offices in Bombay. At twenty-five, it was an intoxication, there's no word more accurate for the city as it was then. The pubs full of intellectuals and artists, dropping their ash into the glasses of those sitting nearby and nobody cared.' One night, a woman at the bar says she is frightened to learn that George and his friend are from India. She knows all about India: a woman called Kali lives there and Indians are her slaves. It is Kali's job to kill people, especially white people, and to drink their blood. She has learned this from an informative book about the country. Late in the evening, after several pints, she agrees that there are at least two slaves of Kali who prefer German beer to English blood.

The SS *Jalakanya* docks in London in June, two weeks after the coronation of Elizabeth II. He wanders around the streets with the familiar names, looking at the buntings and decorations that are yet to be taken down. The mood in the city is celebratory, particularly among labourers and odd-job men. But the drinkers at the pubs are less elated. Their talk is muted and heavy with self-knowledge. They say the pageantry and excess is an indication that England is on the wane as an imperial power.

'I didn't expect the buildings to be a disappointment,' writes George, 'but they were only as impressive as Bombay's Victorian structures. Perhaps my expectations were too high. There was nothing palatial or royal about Buckingham Palace. Just an unremarkable pile of a building.' He then quotes Aldous Huxley, who said the Taj Mahal was not pretty. In that case, how unpretty is Buckingham Palace?

He returns to Bombay, to the *Free Press*. He becomes a father. Sadanand dies – early, he is not yet fifty – and the newspaper seems to lose some of its urgency and glamour. His colleagues no longer appear to him as figures out of an adventure story, but as they are. Ordinary men, without romance. It is time to go. He takes up the editorship of *The Searchlight* and moves the family to the Pataliputra Housing Colony in Patna, towards the north-east. Three weeks after Ammu has set up home, a team of policemen arrive at six-thirty in the morning. George is dressed and waiting. Oddly apologetic, the policemen stand

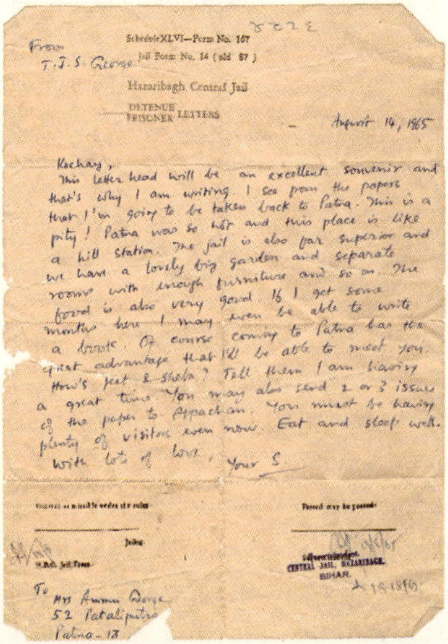

From
T. J. S. George

Schedule XLVI—Form No. 157
Jail Form No. 14 (old 87)

Hazaribagh Central Jail

DETENUE / PRISONER LETTERS

August 14, 1965

Kochay,
This letter head will be an excellent souvenir and
that's why I am writing. I see from the papers
that I'm going to be taken back to Patna. This is a
pity! Patna was so hot and this place is like
a hill station. The jail is also far superior and
we have a lovely big garden and separate
rooms with enough furniture and so on. The
food is also very good. If I get some
months here I may even be able to write
a book. Of course coming to Patna has the
great advantage that I'll be able to meet you.
How's Jeet & Sheba? Tell them I am having
a great time. You may also send 2 or 3 issues
of the paper to Appachan. You must be having
plenty of visitors even now. Eat and sleep well.
With lots of love,
Your S

Superintendent,
CENTRAL JAIL, HAZARIBAGH,
BIHAR.

To
Mrs Ammu George
52 Pataliputra
Patna-13

outside until he emerges. The last we see of him, he is sitting between two uniformed men in the back of a jeep, waving goodbye, looking unreasonably cheerful. It isn't the last time I'll see him disappear in a car.

When the police knock on the door a little after dawn, Ammu panics. Not knowing how to tell her he is being arrested, George has written a letter that he says will explain everything. Waiting on her pillow, it says there was a phone call the previous evening from a friend in the judiciary who informed him he was to be arrested in the morning. There are helpful tips about what she should do in his absence, whom she can ask for help, legal steps to take. Most importantly, she is not to worry because worry is unproductive and the children need her. That is all. There's no mention about why he has been arrested.

At the lock-up in Patna, he's allowed a cell to himself and meals from home. Two weeks later, he is moved to the Hazaribagh Central Jail. He writes to Ammu on prison paper stamped by the jail's superintendent, dated August 14, 1965. George is thirty-seven, the age at which folly gives way to caution. The letter's intent is to allay his wife's fears.

> *Kochay,*
> *This letterhead will be an excellent souvenir and that's why I am writing. I see from the papers that I'm going to be taken back to Patna. A pity! Patna was so hot and this place is like a hill station. The jail is also far superior and we have a lovely big garden and separate rooms with enough furniture and so on. If I get some months here I may even be able to write a book. Of course coming to Patna has the great advantage that I'll be able to meet you. How are Jeet and Sheba? Tell them I am having a great time...*

Years later, when I ask him why he'd been arrested, his answer is typical of someone descended from a long line of silent men: 'I sent some reporters to cover a students' protest and the chief minister didn't like it.'

There's much more to it.

The Pataliputra Housing Colony consists of two blocks designed in the Soviet style. Unadorned concrete exposed to the sun. As editor of Bihar's main English-language newspaper, George is given an apartment on the ground floor. The small bedroom accommodates a bed and almirah, nothing more. His desk is in the front room, the largest in the house, which becomes a meeting place for the student leaders George wants to interview for a series of articles about the protests that have roiled the state.

One is a bespectacled young man with a marked resemblance to the short-story writer Manto. His black horn rims seem to have been borrowed from the costume department of a movie studio. His friend's sparse beard looks borrowed too, tufts of hair that might have been pasted on the man's sunken cheeks. They are offered tea and snacks, which they wolf down. They have questions about Bombay, in particular the film industry and its best-known stars. Is it true that Lata Mangeshkar is driven around in a Cadillac? Hardly the car of choice for the everywoman nightingale of India. And does Guru Dutt actually drive a Jaguar? They are disappointed to hear both rumours are true.

George brings up Chief Minister K.B. Sahay's accusation that the student protesters have engaged in arson and murder.

'Not true, not true,' says Manto. 'Lies! A clear sign of his desperation. Why would we set fire to our own house?'

'I was wondering the same thing.'

'Much worse, mind you, is the other lie, that we're eve-teasers.'

Both men are outraged at the slander.

'What *are* your demands?'

'We want him to listen to us. Number one, just listen.'

The other student, Manto's colleague, blows on the surface of his tea and says between gulps, 'We're only doing what students do, sir, we're protesting against injustice.'

'And the chief minister's charge that you are pro-Pakistani and pro-Peking?'

At this, both men look so bewildered that it comes to George in an instant what he will do. Let them speak in his newspaper.

The Searchlight announces an essay competition on the front page: 'Unrest on the Campus: Reasons & Remedies'. Hundreds of entries arrive, some typewritten, most handwritten. Some are incoherent, others impossible to decipher. The winning essays are published as a booklet, *Student Unrest in Bihar: April 1964*. In the foreword, George writes that it is important to let the students describe in their own words the problems they face.

The booklet is an insight into the caste hierarchy that has survived unchanged through the Indian centuries. It has always existed. It will always exist. However modern and urbane the Indian, the Indian is casteist. The Indian cannot help it.

Christine Massey of St Xavier's College, Ranchi, writes: *I believe that if there were a stiff entrance examination, not only would the quality of the future intelligentsia improve, but unrest in the campus would lessen. I do not believe that a person is qualified for a scholarship merely because he belongs to a former 'backward' or 'suppressed' class.*

The primary cause of India's ills is one we shall have to skip over as no amount of talking will ever remove it, writes Azhar Kalim (who doesn't skip over it). *It is a tragedy too deep for tears how the soul of religion is being asphyxiated by its outer form of convention and custom.*

One upper-caste student, firmly on the side of the authorities, pleads for the censorship of cinema. *Most of these films are based on sex,* writes Rajiv Ranjan Singh. *Students are badly influenced by such films. It's up to the government to check the production of unsocial and unhealthy cinema.* Similarly, books. His suggestion: *Unhealthy literature, which the students of today run after so much, may be banned with advantage by the government.*

(Successive governments are happy to oblige, banning all manner of novels, social studies, travel books, speeches and movies for 'causing hurt to religious sentiments'.)

The booklet's first-person student viewpoints and the editorials in *The Searchlight* are too much for the state government. Chief Minister Sahay announces that the editor's interest in the student agitation amounts to insurrection. The arrest causes an uproar and makes George quickly famous. Telegrams arrive from India and around the world. A case is filed on his behalf by the future defence minister, Krishna Menon. There are protests by journalists in Bombay and Delhi. Editorials defend his right to free speech. The boredom of prison gives him time to think. He doesn't write a book, but he writes letters and an essay, 'Revolt in Bihar: A Study of the August 1965 Uprising', which begins with 'An Explanatory Note': *This report was written in jail. Coming out, I abandoned it because a war had been thrust on us and it was no time for an Indian to turn the searchlight of criticism inward.* The use of *searchlight* is George being playful, and the reference is to war against Pakistan and

China. The essay ends philosophically: *It may be too much to expect self-centred provincial politicians to bother about the content of democracy and the needs of tomorrow: a river cannot rise above its source.*

On the day of his release, Ammu and a group of students, Manto included, wait to greet him. Among the students, there is an air of celebration. George has prepared for the occasion. His beard is trimmed and suit pressed. He looks straight into the camera.

Today, the arrest of journalists and students under the charge of sedition is commonplace. Hardly worth remarking. Oh, a journalist in jail? Right, and what price tomatoes? Outrageous, outrageous! For a kilo? What means this nonsense! It hasn't always been this way. As the first editor of independent India to be charged with sedition, notoriety, fame and unemployability come to him all at once. He cannot continue in Bihar. There is nothing for it but to resign.

It is that time again, time to go.

YEAR OF THE FIRE SHEEP

Hong Kong, 1967

'Oh,' she said, 'that's only Mr Muckerji – a Hindu gentleman. He's not like the other Indian downstairs. Mr Muckerji's very respectful ... He's inquisitive, that's the only thing. Asks such questions.'

'What sort of questions?'

'Oh, everything. Do I believe in horoscopes? Do I believe the newspapers? What do I think of Mr Eden? And he writes down the answers too. I don't know why.'

'Odd.'

... A bell began to ring furiously down below.

She said, 'Oh, he's rightly called Row.'

'Who is?'

'The Indian on the second floor.'

GRAHAM GREENE, ***The Confidential Agent***

PASSPORT
REPUBLIC OF INDIA

WE MOVE FROM A FORMER British colony to one with thirty years left on its lease. The seven-hour flight from Bombay's Sahar airport to Kai Tak in Hong Kong leaves us at a far remove on an island in the South China Sea. Yet, there is no sense of difference. Everyone is from Elsewhere. Our understanding of the people we meet is tribal. We are drawn to those whose experiences mirror our own. Migrants and emigrants, post-colonials, the displaced, those who've been set apart by history or pigmentation and are looking for refuge. That loss of place (the defeat/suppression/end of place) fits the losses of our own extended, scattered family.

On that first journey, as a child of eight, my passport is a flat, cardboard-encased document, too large to fit into a pocket. Over time, there are six others. Each move in search of better is primed for failure. The realization comes late, but fully formed. Displacement creates meaning – and dissolves it. Movement is the message. *Move on.* You lose: you gain.

AMMU FINDS AN APARTMENT HALFWAY up the Peak, on McDonnell Road in the Mid-Levels, a residential area of winding roads and new buildings that houses European expatriates and Chinese business families. She dislikes the city at first, it's so different from anything she has known. The people are rude and in a hurry: they are in a hurry to be rude. There is never time for leisurely conversation or pleasantries of any kind. It is all business, all the time. But soon she begins to enjoy watching the seasons change from the balcony of the fourth-floor apartment. Behind the building are thick woods that lead up to Bowen Road, lush green in the summer, transformed by the brief cold winter into dead leaves and brush. When they take the Star Ferry to visit the shiny emporiums of Nathan Road, less expensive than the department stores on the island, she feels the change as winter deepens. The sharp wind brings tears to her eyes as she stands by the rail and watches Kowloon take shape in the distance, waterline melding into urban skyline, into rural blight, into the vast forbidden reaches of China. Her light Delhi sweater is useless against the chill off the water. At Daimaru, she finds padded Chinese jackets for the children, light, surprisingly warm, with handmade buttons and dragon patterns on the red, blue and black silk. She buys space heaters and thermal underwear. The first Cantonese phrase she learns is *Kay tho cheena?* The question is inevitable at the street stalls in Central where she buys soaps, towels, toothbrushes and clothes. It is the correct way of starting the ritual of negotiation that attends any kind of purchase in Hong Kong. *How much?* Because everything is negotiable and bargaining is an art, a teachable skill that the shopkeepers insist on and clearly enjoy. At the first price they quote, she always frowns and shakes her head as if in disbelief at the hawker's mendacity. The final price is always substantially lower than the opening salvo. She learns to take pleasure in the transaction, the way the shopkeepers adjust their attitudes when she begins to bargain, their new respect at her shrewdness. But at Daimaru, these newly acquired skills do not matter. The prices are fixed and surprisingly reasonable. She picks out a red silk jacket for her daughter and one of black silk for her son. For George, she buys no clothes. He prefers to have his jackets made to measure at a tailor who stitches the customer's name and his own on the inside pocket: *T J George, Carlton Tailor, Causeway Bay*.

In the pageantry of the island, unfolding district by district, Ammu experiences Elsewhere as a spiritual calling. Among crowds of people of every race and religion, she knows internationalism as the true nationalism and freedom as the only patriotism.

Over dinner at the Foreign Correspondents' Club, at the round dining tables and the great circular bar, are people as new to Hong Kong as she. There are new friends, the closest of whom is also from Kerala, a small, clever woman named Prasanna, mother of two, who moved first to the Philippines, then to Hong Kong when her husband took a job with the *South China Morning Post*. It is a pleasure to speak with her in Malayalam and to find that their conversation fits easily with the other languages on the streets: Tagalog, Hindi, Mandarin, English, Dutch, Indonesian. With Prasanna, she discovers the lanes of Central and the staircase markets that run like umbilical cords between Queen's Road Central and the Mid-Levels. They find seasonal clothing, vegetable vendors, repair shops, electronic goods, and basic lessons in spoken Cantonese. In the wet market are items she would never have thought of as food, fried chicken feet with the skin puckered and orange, scaled razor-toothed sea monsters, dogs in cages.

Tucked into a landing off the Pottinger Street staircase, they find a sign that says, in English, FREE STOCK MARKET TIPS. A long-haired young man in sunglasses and bell-bottoms speaks from the cash counter of a small noodle shop jammed with people. Ammu and Prasanna nurse jasmine tea in short water glasses and listen intently.

'My name is Homer Wai Pang. I don't want to speak metaphor, okay! I want to speak literal,' says the man, who then speaks mainly in metaphors. 'Everybody knows Hong Kong Stock Market deals in equity of listed companies. It buys and sells small parcels of equity! If you buy parcel, let's call it share, then you own part of company for as long as you hold on to share. Following me? Okay! Shares increase or decrease according to demand. Think of it like parcel of food at noodle shop. If many people are waiting in line to buy, day after day, the shopkeeper will do one or two thing. He will become proud and rude, or he will increase price of noodles. Correct? When price decreases, bargain hunters move in to buy. When price increases, profit hunters sell, causing price to drop again.'

Homer takes a coin out of his pocket, flips it in the air and slams it on the counter. 'Heads or tails?' There is a small show of hands for heads and an equally modest count for tails. 'Okay, you see? Half people in this room wrong,' he says, pocketing the coin without showing its face. He crosses his arms and smoothes his sparse beard. 'There are two kinds investors. Gambling man, prudent man. Gambling man buys shares in brand-new company. When share move up and down quickly, he buys and sells. Prudent man buys shares in banking or life insurance or oil. He waits. Patience! Decide who you are, okay.'

Ammu puts down her glass and turns to her friend. They are in the crush by the cash counter. She is happy nobody around her understands Malayalam.

'Prasanna, Prasanna, why is he doing it?'

'Doing what, Ammu, making us rich?'

'Why is he giving free advice?'

Prasanna points to the small print under the FREE TIPS sign. 'To make us join the advanced class at thirty-nine dollars per session!'

Homer picks up a Cantonese-language newspaper and points to a front-page story well above the fold. 'See this? If you been looking at Hang Seng Index on Wednesday, you must have notice market was suffering from vertigo after dramatic three-hundred-point jump. So okay! You buy or sell? You want vertigo or not? Decide quick! Me? I'm gambler.'

Ammu says, in whispered Malayalam, 'Forget the advanced course. Better not to be a gambler. Better we put the thirty-nine dollars in Hong Kong and Shanghai Bank!'

As it turns out, they put twenty-five thousand dollars each into the bank. When it pays off, they invest the same amount again. When the market goes into vertigo, they sell. Like Ammu, Prasanna is also married to a journalist with no interest in money. While the men work and give their salaries to their wives, the two women find ways to make the money grow. During the boom years of the Hong Kong Stock Exchange, they make enough to invest in several small parcels, not of shares but of real estate. In one particularly profitable week, they visit each of the four stock exchanges and watch the frenzy wide-eyed, feeling some small amount of pride, the only women wearing saris among a sea of red blazers. Ammu takes to monitoring her investments daily, sometimes twice daily. George says she is addicted to the market and somehow it pleases her to hear this.

The following year, with not a word of warning, the market crashes.

The children are at school and George is at work. From the kitchen window, she can see the thick woods on the hill behind the building and a stretch of McDonnell Road that appears wet and shiny in the shimmer. The sky is weirdly white, not a shred of blue, and there is a metallic shine in the air. She has forgone her free hour before lunch because the ayah asked to come early that day. The woman is needed that afternoon to cook for a party at the Macadams' on the third floor. Ammu fries banana fritters for tea and makes a salad of cabbage, grated coconut, green chilli and leftover peanut chutney. She is teaching Ah Sing how to make a Kerala red fish curry when the woman brings that morning's *Hong Kong Standard* from the front room to wrap the fish entrails and scales. Which is when Ammu remembers that she hasn't seen the day's paper. Which is when she notices the headline that makes her stop and place the fish knife very carefully in the sink. It is the top story, screaming headlines in tall forbidding Biblical letters: 'MARKETS CRASH. HANG SENG INDEX IN FREE FALL'. Her stomach goes into free fall first, then her heart. The first thing she does is to call Prasanna. At one o'clock, she is waiting at the bus stand on Des Voeux Road, and when Prasanna alights the two women walk grimly to the noodle shop. Homer cannot be found. The proprietor speaks lightly of suicide or murder or worse.

'Castle Peak,' he says, using the local phrase for 'psycho'. The man makes a circular motion with index finger pointed at temple, laughing to indicate it is a joke. Castle Peak is the island's mental hospital, spread over forty sprawling acres. 'Today, so many finance people have nervous breakdown Castle Peak has its own stock exchange and broker! Wai Pang must be there!'

When she gets home, the ayah's fish curry stands glutinous and oil-streaked on the kitchen counter. The children are watching *Hawaii Five-O* in the living room, her son standing upside down on the couch, feet balanced against a Ho Chi Minh poster. When George gets home, they gather at the dining table.

'What is that?' asks her son with a voice full of apprehension.

'Yeah, what?' says her daughter.

'Fish curry, I taught Ah Sing how to make it,' says Ammu.

'No,' says her son. 'Please, no. How can?'

She serves him a spoonful of the glistening curry.

Her son prods a chunk of fish with a fork, then places everything else on his plate at a far remove from the red substance, as if it were contagious. He eats everything but refuses to touch or look at the fish.

'Finish your food,' says George, ominously calm.

'I can't,' says her son. 'It causes deep damage. You don't understand.'

'Understand this,' says George. 'You won't leave the table until you finish everything on your plate.'

The silence is deep and personal after they finish dinner and Ammu clears the dishes. Her son's plate stays on the table, the shrunken fish slimy and dull. The boy sits there for two hours, staring straight ahead, refusing to look at the red matter on his plate, as stubborn as his father. At intervals, he speaks to himself. The word 'damage' and 'act of God' can be heard. At eleven-thirty, he is still there, prepared to stay all night if necessary. Unable to bear it any longer, Ammu goes to him and puts out her hand without a word. Her son gives her three pieces of fish, which she deposits quickly in the trash.

'He's finished,' she tells George, who is watching the news.

The boy is allowed to go to bed.

That night, lying awake in the dark, she comes to a decision. She will not sell her newly worthless shares. In her mind, the sixty thousand dollars she's put into the treacherous, disloyal stock market, every last cent of it, is money George has earned from long hours of work and tireless sacrifice. She feels pangs of guilt when she remembers how recklessly, how *wantonly* she wasted so much money. But it is important to remember that it isn't lost just yet. It is important not to panic. It is important to keep a level head, fight fate with patience. She knows how to wait. She'll outwait the downturn, no, say it, *the crash*. She'll keep waiting however long it takes.

It so happens she waits four and a half years, until the market rights itself. She then sells at a decent profit. While the saga plays itself out, George says nothing, not a word of reprimand. To him, the stock market, money in general, is a kind of abstraction. There is nothing there.

AFTERWARDS, HE WILL REMEMBER HONG KONG as a puzzlement. Did he really do those audacious things on that curious island? They say it is tiny, but it never seems so to him. Their first apartment is on Robinson Road, in a building with an odd name: Arts Mansion. No art to be seen anywhere, except a pair of rusted flamingoes in the lobby. The winding roads stretch all the way up to the luxury houses at the Peak. From there, residential spaces descend in order of wealth until they turn into squalid one-room apartments on the housing estates of Mongkok and the rural tenements of the New Territories. Between the Arts Mansion flat and the offices of the *Far Eastern Economic Review* in Central, the island is a world unto itself, unknown and therefore vast.

Another puzzle is the absence of water. In the early days, he isn't fully convinced it is an island. Unlike Bombay where the sea is always present, in Hong Kong no water is to be seen unless he and Ammu take the ferry to Kowloon. And then it is a short stretch, a moat, an apron of water between mainland and island, dwarfed by tall ships and taller buildings. And it *is* tiny: fifty-five square miles. A colonial leaseholding that has entered the last three decades of its ninety-nine-year term as a Crown colony. Englishmen make up the governors, high judges, school principals, senior police officers, television anchors and journalists. His new job has taken him from the chaos of the former empire to a dot in the South China Sea. In his mind, he has at last arrived in the world, far away from his beginnings.

To make it clear he is Asian not Caucasian, he changes his byline from T.J.S. George to Thayil Jacob Sony George. He grows his hair and keeps a goatee, orders paisley shirts from India and waistcoats from a tailor in Causeway Bay. Psychedelic flyers appear in the living room. A framed portrait of Nietzsche on the kitchen counter. A Proudhon poster above the dining table. The French anarchist wears blue jeans and an artist's smock and there are speech bubbles: *Property is theft! Ownership is slavery!* He buys an Akai 4000DS reel-to-reel machine and the house rings to Captain Beefheart, the Plastic Ono Band, Janis Joplin, The Jimi Hendrix Experience, Tangerine Dream, T-Rex, Sly and the Family Stone. But the reel-to-reel plays only when they have guests. Otherwise, he likes silence, music interferes with writing.

On the second or third day, it strikes him. He is the only brown man in the office. Like wearing a badge of some sort, a uniform that sets him apart once and forever. The *Review*'s mission is Asia, but Englishmen and Australians make up the senior staff. They render Asia eccentrically, as a source of humour or weirdness. The magazine seems to address readers in London or New York or Frankfurt, anywhere but an Asian city. As regional editor, his job is to write opinion pieces on Southeast

Asian leaders and ASEAN conclaves. The jokey edits and columns about 'exotic' local passions – like the 'Traveller's Tales' feature on the back page – are written by editor-in-chief Derek Davies and a cabal that favours three-piece suits and ascots.

Among his colleagues, some are colour-blind. He is setting up his portable typewriter when a tall, gangly man introduces himself. Michael O'Neill, New Zealander. His height and stoop give him a slightly supercilious air. Unfounded, as it turns out. O'Neill is supercilious only when faced with pomposity. They assess each other for a moment in silence. Something is decided at that moment. Their collaboration will come to define their professional lives.

'Never trust a man who smokes footlongs,' says Mike, indicating the editor's cabin where Davies and the advertising heads are puffing on afternoon stogies.

'Not even if the cigars are Cuban?'

'Most especially not if the cigars are Cuban.'

George notes that the bearded O'Neill speaks around a briar clenched between his teeth. He seems much older than his rumoured years.

'Is it true what they say, that you're twenty-six?'

'It is indeed.'

'And that you dropped out of school at sixteen to become a newspaperman?'

'Absolutely not! I joined the oldest, most venerable daily in New Zealand, the *Taranaki Herald* out of New Plymouth, at age fifteen.'

'And here you are at Hong Kong's oldest British periodical.'

'It isn't easy, you know. New Zealanders are Asians, southerners, pretty much as south as you can get,' says Mike. Then he nods at the editor's cabin. 'I keep telling the suits, but they don't understand.'

The suits. As if it were a new caste. Being an Indian resident in Hong Kong makes you sensitive to such distinctions. The Cantonese take their racial hierarchies seriously. Europeans are on top, Hong Kong Chinese next, Indians somewhere at the bottom, along with Pakistanis, Arabs and Filipinos. The Cantonese have an epithet for Indian, *Yan do*, pronounced in a tone dripping with dislike. He hears it often, in the bazaars and on the street. It doesn't rankle because the Cantonese are equal-opportunity racists. Their phrase for the white man, *Gwei lo*, is also uttered in tones of revulsion, with an added hit of superstitious fear. No, what rankles is the British word for Indians, *Bhangis*. Malicious empathy, to know what will bother a caste-obsessed people the most, to choose a caste of sweepers, toilet-cleaners and corpse-handlers, and then apply the word to all Indians. Genius! A profound understanding of how to get under a people's skin. British ingenuity at its creative peak. He can't help but admire it.

In the weeks that follow, George and Mike take to lunching at the modest establishments that dot Central and Causeway Bay. When they have the funds, they go to the Foreign Correspondents' Club at Sutherland House, near the Central waterfront, or to Fook Lam Moon on Johnston Road. Later, trying to recall the exact sequence of events, George is certain that it was at Fook Lam that they came up with the idea of a magazine, a new kind of journalism, new in the context of Hong Kong if nowhere else: Asia interpreting itself without supervision from the West.

Over sweet-and-sour pork, Cantonese fried rice and dim sum, they think up the slogan: *Asia through Asian eyes.*

'Revolutionary.'

'Incendiary. The suits might have a fit.'

Over lychee ice cream and coffee, much too much coffee, they craft a mission statement: *To report accurately and fairly the affairs of Asia in all spheres of human activity, to see the world from an Asian perspective, to be Asia's voice in the world.*

They resign at the same time. George goes to New York, where he works as a writer with the United Nations World Population Year. The family moves into a twelfth-floor apartment on Seventy-Ninth and York, with a view of the canyons and ravines of glass and steel, the blank windows as far as the eye can see. Mike goes to the Philippines to set up a news agency. Meanwhile, they raise money. A year and a half after leaving the *Review*, they return to Hong Kong. Word spreads. Mike finds cheap offices in Wanchai on the humid fringe of the red-light district, next door to the Suzie Wong clubs and the hangouts of triad bosses. *Fragrant* is the word. It takes all of three weeks to hire a band of writers, photographers and illustrators – and they are in business.

The first issue of *Asiaweek* appears in 1975. Singapore, Malaysia, Thailand, Indonesia and the Philippines are economies on the verge. It is lucky timing. The slogan thought up at Fook Lam Moon is rendered into flesh. In the editorial, George writes, 'It is now a new Asia, and this is a new magazine to report it.'

They move into bigger offices. They hire better talent. They make money, and then they make a mistake. Looking to expand, they sell a majority share to *Reader's Digest*, which is sold on to Time Inc. for several million dollars. None of the money comes to *Asiaweek*. In 1981, George leaves his share of the magazine to Mike and returns to Bombay.

Disaster follows.

'Fine editorial this week,' says a Time Inc. man in the elevator as they go down for lunch one day.

'Thanks,' Mike replies. 'But how can you tell?'

If he has endeared himself to the Asians on staff, he's done the very opposite with the new American owners. After twenty years of work on the magazine he helped to found, Mike is fired. Then they shut it down.

'Perhaps that had been the intention all along,' says George during his bad moments. 'Total monopoly.'

They were outsiders, he and Mike. They had no network, no sponsors, no unlimited supply of funds. All they had was the magazine they'd created, which now had a circulation of 130,000 copies. Yet, this creation, this perfectly healthy entity, had been extinguished. If he dwells on what had happened, the injustice hits him in waves. Why had they not offered the magazine for sale if it was unprofitable? Why say it was losing money when it was not? Insult upon injury to shut it down and delete the *Asiaweek* articles and images, built up over decades, from *Time*'s online archives. They know the real reason. The magazine was killed in an attempt to revive *Time Asia*, the comatose entity whose owners saw *Asiaweek* as chief competitor and threat.

Mike moves to the Philippines, where his wife has a home. Without a job, it is impossible to live on the island where rents are among the highest in the world. Consumed by notions of conspiracy, mourning the loss of the magazine they had built from nothing more than an idea, he decides to take Time Inc. to court. He is in the midst of a long legal anxiety when he dies of a heart attack at the age of forty-nine.

The dream of a new Asian journalism has been killed, not by time, the usual assassin of men and magazines, but by *Time*.

HE'S BACK IN INDIA AFTER FOURTEEN YEARS. With what feelings? Oh, nervousness, surely. And hope. The economic model of planned socialism has run itself into the sand. Reform is in the air. They land in Bombay on a Friday night, and by Sunday Ammu makes liveable the Bandra flat they'd bought years earlier, a spacious dwelling with a six-inch view of the sea. He'll get started on the novel he's been meaning to write since the age of eighteen. Now, he has the means.

On Monday morning, he commutes from the bedroom to the living room and puts a sheet of foolscap into his Underwood and types the line he's committed to memory, the first line he's been carrying in his head for the better part of a decade: *This is a tale told by an unborn child.* He waits for the next line. But without a deadline and no one waiting for his copy, with the uncertainty as to when or if the words will ever appear in print, it isn't easy to get on. The uncertainty, that's the thing. What does it matter if he finishes? Who will notice? But he keeps at it, writing two or three hundred words a day, and hating himself, his speed all wrong for a journalist used to writing two thousand words on the spot. Where's the urgency? Dead like the prose. By the end of the month, he has six chapters stiff to the touch. Not a real sentence in the lot. Meanwhile, the novels, his talismans, sit on the shelf and regard him balefully. He gives up reading, forgets his earliest ambition. The fame he won all those years ago hasn't translated into a literary career.

Some days, he doesn't get out of bed. Ammu says nothing. It is his son who asks what is wrong. Exactly the kind of question he'd never have asked of his own father. What can be said in response? And there's the other thing. Although they don't have rent to pay, there are monthly maintenance amounts. College fees are due for his son and school fees for his daughter, dues for furniture, fuel, groceries and medicine. One morning, the phone rings, a friend he'd worked with in Bombay who's now the editor of a Delhi newspaper, *Indian Express*.

'Write a column for us,' says his friend.

'A column,' he says, looking at the two paragraphs he wrote the week before. 'Well, what about?'

'I don't know,' says his friend. In the background, the sound of a typewriter, which, for him, is the sound of someone fighting extinction, the addictive rhythm he hasn't heard in who knows how long? 'How about, let's see, anything you want?'

He spends much of his time prone, staring into the distance. One morning, alarmed to find him in bed with no plans for the day or the days to come, his son thinks to talk to him. But he's forgotten that his father never speaks about his problems, only his son's. He asks for no advice, he only offers it. He rarely speaks at all. It is one of the reasons they've never been close.

'What's wrong?' asks his son.

George picks up a newspaper and pretends to read.

'What makes you think something's wrong? Everything is fine. I'm reading...'

'No, you're not.'

'You can't write if you don't read. Writers read differently from other people. My reading isn't passive. It's active.'

He doesn't look very active. He is sprawled on the bed in his nightclothes, piles of newspapers around him. His typewriter is back in its case. There are no notebooks or pens to be seen.

'I'm reading Mandelstam's poems,' his son says when the silence threatens to drown them.

'Russian?'

'Yes.'

He pulls his newspaper down and speaks over the crumpled pages.

'Don't waste your time on poetry, there's no profit in it. Read Bertrand Russell and C.E.M. Joad, Orwell, Graham Greene. Read Somerset Maugham. John le Carré. Write a novel if you want to be a writer.'

His son can't reply but stands rooted to his spot in the middle of the bedroom. *No profit in poetry*. It's the kind of thing you'd expect from an accountant or shopkeeper, from a plumber, a second-hand car salesman. As for the reading list, George may have started a magazine whose mission was to return Asia to Asians, but his literary idols were firmly colonial. Maybe he senses what is on his son's mind.

'I brought these with me,' he says, gesturing to a pile of books scattered on the unmade bed. The authors he mentioned are all there.

His talismans. Beacon lights for the books he hopes to write some day. 'But lately, I've been having doubts. So much literature, especially great literature, is racially exclusive. Not intended for people like us. I mean brown people. If you were to compile a list…'

'Reading while brown? It would be endless.'

'You'd have to narrow it down. Be selective.'

Through the open window, above the low rooftops of the neighbouring buildings, the light softens and dies. The sky goes purple with streaks of dull gold and it starts lightly to rain.

The heavy silence between them returns and then George speaks in a way his son has never heard. He allows himself to seem vulnerable.

'I have nothing to do, that's all. I might be going through a fallow patch. It can happen to anyone.'

'But it hasn't happened to you before.'

'Maybe it's a question of getting acclimatized to India again. I don't know. I'm waiting for something.'

It strikes his son later that George was in the midst of a depression. He'd returned to the backwaters, far away from the great cities of the world. It would have been a rough homecoming. *I might be going through a fallow patch*. For a man of his pride, it was as if he'd admitted to a moral failing.

He becomes a distressing presence around whom the household adjusts itself. He reads the newspapers and stays in bed for much of the day. Sometimes, he takes a chair to the window and gazes at the palm trees. There are mysterious phone calls. A business trip to Bangalore.

'He's embarrassed to apply for jobs,' Ammu says. 'He wants someone to make him an offer.'

Two months after his return, someone does.

George becomes the editor of *The Times of Deccan*. A badly produced broadsheet full of local news and no advertisements, funded by a politician who expects immediate profits when there are none to be had. Money is a constant worry. Somehow the staff is paid. As editor, George receives no salary. One afternoon, the politician-proprietor appears, his aide shuts the door of the editor's cabin and produces a bundle of cash. It is the only payment George will receive. A year later, he resigns and the newspaper shuts down. He begins a Sunday column for the *Indian Express* that will continue without a break for twenty-five years. He is of the Gandhian generation, embarrassed by money and exalted by idealism. He asks for, and receives, a monthly salary of a thousand and one rupees.

CHUNGKING NIGHTS

Hong Kong, 1997

This note is a Remarkable Rhetorical Device. Unlike, say, the diacope or an arithmetic progression or chiasmus or anaphora, this device is not designed to stagger your attention, break it into pieces, and turn it back on itself, rather, it is here to make you complicit in the argument on offer, that control can be freedom, and that a patchwork composite is more effective than its linear, chronological opposite.

A BURMESE CAT SLIPS PAST the water-stained concrete at the end of the pier. Repulse Bay. A middling million-dollar beach with rowboats and yachts tucked snug against the pilings. Rowing in the dark, I make for the last junk on the right. 'Look for the blue one,' Whit had said, 'you'll find it, there's no other boat that colour.' But it's long past midnight and everything is blue. Blue light dripping down the sky. Long blue shadows on the water. Blue disc of moon riding the swells. There are no lights burning on the junks at anchor. No lights in the harbour but reflected starlight. I row and rest, row and bump up against the junk and secure the rowboat. Below deck, a narrow cabin and a bunk. I wake to the sound of the open sea. Someone has set sail while I was sleeping. People are everywhere, holidaymakers getting a start on Christmas Eve. A man in a costume captain hat pours from a magnum bottle. Behind him, a glimpse of the island, already at an impossible distance. Accidental stowaway on the wrong junk. At sea, at sea. No surprise there. Just another mistake in a decade full of them.

'You're welcome to help with the sail if you feel like,' says the captain. 'Have some wine!'

'Thanks for letting me stay.'

'No need to thank. Where you from?'

'India.'

'British colony! We have something in common.'

'Your freedom is new, though.'

'Freedom? We were British possession. Now we're Chinese possession.

Our island is shining example of one country, two system. If Deng Xiao Ping says so, it must be true. Am I right or wrong?'

He waves off a waiter bearing glisteningly unidentifiable canapés.

'Prosperity, education, freedom. All promises fulfilled! Especially freedom!' He picks up his champagne but doesn't drink. 'Anyway, we can look forward to 2047. Expiry of one country, two system.'

'Long time to wait.'

'In 1898, ninety-nine years seemed like forever. It's nothing. This is fifty years, less than nothing.' He downs the champagne like a shot. 'But never mind. Tonight there's a tailwind. We celebrate.'

He has become a displaced person without leaving the island. I have become displaced by returning and taking a job with *Asiaweek*.

Here's something I'd like to share. I was ready to quit the week I started work. Under Time Inc., the only thing the magazine has in common with the one George and Mike founded more than twenty years earlier is the name. It is now a steamy fug of petty intrigue. Turncoats and spies abound. There are factions. You have to know who is who. As the son of the former founder, I won't be popular. Except maybe with some dissident outfit looking to burn down the house.

I report to an editor George had hired. An ethnic Indian from a well-known Hong Kong Muslim family. Smarmily, smilingly he's ingratiated himself with the new management. And makes it a point to display in his office Salman Rushdie's *The Satanic Verses*. He hasn't read the book. Of this we are all certain. It is a way of establishing his secular cred.

In his office, I express a mild opinion about the novel, something about its value as a piece of literary scholarship.

'No,' he says, fixed smile gone rictus.

I suggest a story for the next issue about small businesses being driven out by multinational chains. Off the top of my head, I can think of nothing less anodyne.

'No,' he says. 'No, no.'

'Your favourite word in all the world.'

'Yes.'

'Okay, but,' I say, my eyes straying to the untouched Rushdie spine-outward by his computer, 'I'd like to pitch it at the meeting.'

'No. We're a business magazine now. No human-interest features, no frothy opinion pieces, no arts, no reviews. Follow the money.'

He mouths the last phrase in all seriousness, subverting the advice of a pair of journalists who brought down an American president.

I don't plan to stay, so I don't rent an apartment. I live in hotels or sleep on couches. When Whit returns to the office after his Christmas holiday, I move into Chungking Mansions on Nathan Road. There, a traveller will find a home for a night or a hundred nights, however unstable his circumstances. I am happy enough with a bed that doesn't buck all night like the bunk bed on a junk.

After work, I take a late bowl of tofu and noodle soup at a stall on the first floor operated by a man who is his own cook, waiter, cashier and cleaning staff. His stall, which is little more than a booth, displays a bright selection of handmade soybean items. There is golden tofu and white tofu, cold and sweet tofu milkshakes, tofu of varied textures from firm to melt-in-the-mouth, crispy tofu skin served with a spicy red pepper sauce, paper bowls of almond tofu, slabs of frozen tofu for hotpots, and a special dish available on certain days only, something he calls dirty tofu, an addictive invention flash-fried over a standing stove, the flames leaping into the small wok that has been drizzled liberally with Shaoxing wine. A stick of three pieces of dirty tofu is available for a negligible amount. It is his most popular item and there are all kinds of people standing in line for it, including those who do not live at Chungking Mansions or in Kowloon, who come all the way from the New Territories and from the island. Of course there is another reason for the popularity of his stall. There are rumours that he was once famous as a poet of fortune cookies, then became a favourite of Mao's, and there are customers who come just to have a look at him.

Our first conversation circles round a photograph in the *South China Morning Post*. A trio of women with shopping bags from the designer stores on Nathan Road. Chanel sunglasses and fur coats inappropriate for the weather. The photographer has taken the image from the back, the women walking away from the camera, the picture capturing the open contempt on the faces of the pedestrians who pass. The caption says something about how much mainlanders enjoy shopping on Nathan Road. No mention is made of what Hongkongers think.

'Hongkongers hate mainlanders, it's plain to see,' says the tofu-stall owner, wiping the already clean table.

'Always have, always will.'

'In China, the *People's Daily* said 1984 was the year of great success. Zhao Ziyang visited the United States and Ronald Reagan came to China. But Hong Kong people laughed. They said mainlanders think they're a world power because Americans gave their leader a visa.'

'Hongkongers make a joke about everything. Mostly things they worry about.'

'Must be why they're joking about the Handover. How mainlanders point at a high-rise on the Mid-Levels – far, far up for maximum status – and tell the real estate agent to find them an apartment in *that* building. They don't even want to see. All they want is the title deed.'

'Paint the apartment Chanel pink to go with the heart-shaped bags.'

'Mainlanders don't believe in anything. They want to swallow the island whole.'

'And you,' I ask, 'what do you believe in?'

He gets busy with his next batch of silky tofu. 'This, this I believe.'

'This I believe, too.'

'Chanel, ah? Let me tell you a story.'

Over small bowls of tofu and noodles, tofu and greens, tofu and shrimp, he tells me of his journey to Chungking Mansions, how as a young man he had no idea he would one day leave his ancestral home in China, leave the mainland altogether in a desperate attempt to escape his secret life as the Great Helmsman's pet poet.

When the response came it was exceedingly mild (he says). Only a certain kind of worker would have understood it as a rebuke.

Monday afternoon. I typed up the day's work. On the floor were five usables, nine possibles, and an ever-increasing pile of rejections. I always thought it was a good day when I threw away more than I kept. By that standard it was an exceptional day.

When I looked up, the Factory Superintendent was at the door. A rare and anxiety-causing occasion, that she would visit me and do so without warning. The bile rose into my throat, I'm ashamed to say.

But we who worked in the vineyard of the word, we were cowed by the Cultural Revolution. I thought it was only a matter of time before I too had to submit to the great humiliation. A blackboard around my neck, my name crossed out, announcing to all, family, friends, strangers, that I was a mistake in need of immediate correction.

'Poet Huang,' said the Factory Superintendent. My anxiety grew. She and I had never exchanged a word in all the time I had worked at the factory, and now she was addressing me by name as poet. 'The Director of Printing and Factory Processes wishes to see you.'

Then, smiling mysteriously, she moved closer and whispered that it had something to do with the last batch of fortunes I had written. Perhaps I'd expected such a summons. Perhaps I'd been hoping for some small measure of praise. But now that it had come, I was filled with fear. I followed the Superintendent to the Processes Directorate. In all the years I'd worked at Tipsy Horse Fortune Cookies, this was the first time I'd been summoned to the rooms where every important decision was made, where only the most trusted employees were allowed. As we walked past my co-workers, I wondered what they were thinking. None of them looked at me, none except Shin Shin, the new worker ridiculed by everyone for her high taste in sunglasses.

'Close the door behind you, Factory Superintendent,' said the Director, as if he was in a hurry to talk to me in private.

He said nothing further until the Superintendent had left. But even after the door was shut and we were alone, he said nothing. He stood at the window, staring as if a storm was headed straight for us. A cigarette was burning in his fingers, or I should say it was burning his fingers. It seemed he'd forgotten the Double Happiness until he threw the butt to the floor.

'*Dew lay lo mow-uh*,' he said, looking straight at me. '*Chow hai siu fan hum ka chan-uh*.'

These obscenities were heard everywhere in our city, uttered by schoolchildren and soldiers and peasants. The first part of it insulted the listener's mother and the second promised disaster to his descendants. Still, it was unsettling to hear the Director mouthing curses at me. I stood in the recommended posture, with my back straight and my hands behind me, and pretended I hadn't heard.

'Forgive my language, Comrade Huang, but this is an extraordinary moment,' said the Director.

I said nothing. At that moment, words were beyond me. I felt such confusion that I was convinced the slightest attempt to speak would lead to a fit of vomiting or something more severe, a seizure of some sort.

'Do you know the story of the degenerate French design house, Chanel, Comrade Huang?' the Director asked.

I assured him that I did not.

'Chanel was a ruthless woman and a good leader, you will not be surprised to hear,' said the Director, attempting to smile. 'She made a profitable income from poetry. Can you guess how?'

Not a word came out of my mouth.

'She kept a poet on hand to coin aphorisms for her capitalist empire.'

'Yes, Director,' I said, bewildered by this talk of a Frenchwoman.

'Of course, the aphorisms were attributed to her and no one else,' the Director continued. 'Do you understand?'

'Yes, Director,' I replied dutifully, although I understood nothing.

'Chanel's axiom that luxury is liberty, for example, or that luxury is a necessity ... During the Occupation, she chose the collaborator's path, acquiring a powerful German protector who made sure she did not want for butter and sugar,' said the Director, lighting another Double Happiness.

I tried to mask my confusion by standing straighter.

'But this is all beside the point,' said the Director.

Then he uttered the most startling proposition of my life.

'The Great Leader came across your fortunes in a box of Tipsy Horse cookies presented to him as a gift. He liked one in particular: *Dine not on another's delicacies lest you turn away from your own*. He wants you to send him, in private, a steady number of such aphorisms that you cannot share with anyone, not even the valued managers of Tipsy Horse Fortune Cookies.'

I asked the question burning on my lips: 'Not even you, Director?'

'Not even I, Comrade Huang.'

And so began the worst and best years of my life. I married Shin Shin and we had a daughter. After three and a half years of marriage, my wife took a job as the boss of a soft drink company in Shanghai. She forgot about me. I didn't mind. But I couldn't forgive her for forgetting our daughter.

I wrote hundreds of aphorisms that the Great Leader compiled into a book, into two books, into a collection of little books that made him revered among the people. When I saw one of the books clutched in the hands of a colleague, or a friend, or a stranger on the street, it created in me a depth of loathing I didn't know I possessed. Still, I did as they asked. I wrote. The greater my loathing, the better the aphorism.

I was happy the Leader didn't reprimand me in some way. Or demand my participation at a Speak Bitterness session preliminary to my internment in a labour camp.

But I learned an important lesson.

To wait is to give up. Better to risk everything than do nothing.

When I got the chance, I bought a plane ticket for my daughter to attend a language school in the United States. The reforms had begun. The memory of the labour camps began to fade. I knew better. Soon after the Handover, before they made any changes in the immigration structure, I took a trip through the New Territories to Kowloon. It was to be a one-week visit to see my Auntie Lim and two young cousins.

A friend booked me into this building in Tsim Tsa Tsui that I've made my home for eight months now. 36-44 Nathan Road. Where the world's migrants set up camp and a person can disappear forever if they want. I made tofu, which I used to make as a young man. I became known for the silkiness of my product. Once I make enough money, I'll buy a plane ticket. I'll tell the naturalization officers my story.

My daughter says it's only right I tell them everything.

ISOLATION

Berlin, Elmau, Frankfurt, 2013

'I learned some Italian today.'

'What, in Germany?'

'Yes, yes. Mangia molto, caca forte, non aver paura della morte.'

'What does it mean?'

'Eat plenty, shit well, have no fear of death or hell.'

'Easy for you to say.'

THE GERMAN IS TRAINED. His precise strike leaves me with a black eye that takes a long time to fade. I don't hit back. I sit in my seat and wait for the room to right itself. When it does, the man is gone. I grab a handful of ice from the champagne bucket and hold it to my eye and walk out in search of a taxi.

But let's begin in Kreutzberg at the apartment without colour. All that fall, I wake to milky light. I put the CD on and skip forward to track five and wait for the slow tick of the snare. The lyrics like a religious text: *Where are we now?* The old man making a list of the places he knew when he was young. Potsdamer Platz and Nürnberger Strasse. The Dschungel. KaDeWe. The old man with cancer, speaking from the future. *Just walking the dead.* Track five in the hospital-white apartment. No pictures except the large black-and-white photograph of a munitions factory that looms above my head as I sleep. In the city built to no human scale, those brutal buildings designed to crush the spirit, streets created for the free movement of tanks, avenues that are default runways for small to medium warplanes.

Mornings, chastened, beside myself, I crack open the frigid blinds. Sometimes there is a huddled shape on the street. Impossible to tell if it is a man or a woman. I imagine a transplant, uncomfortable as I but better able to cope with the vile outside. Rain flecks the window with specks of ice. The wind cuts deep. In a day, in two days, in a matter of hours, I come to experience the city as a form of deprivation. I play the prophetic song of songs *Where are we now?* and wait for the coda *As long as there's sun ...* but there is none, not a glimmer. The half-light wavers until two-thirty in the afternoon. Then the sun gives up like the rest of us. Coming from a climate in which the only constant is light, the lack of it is a cruelty. In the city built for sturmtruppen, I take cold comfort in the apartment's white surfaces, the rooms untouched by human hands. Gripped by the sudden flatness that comes over visitors from the tropics in the midst of a European winter, I don't unpack, I eat sparingly, I sleep long hours.

I wake to the phone.

'Boy, there's something to tell you.'

My mother calling from India, loud enough to be heard across continents.

'This doesn't sound good.'

'It's not good. Appa has prostate cancer.'

'Oh no.'

'But it's treatable and he's taking the medication. He wants to talk to you. I'll give him the phone.' Bad-news calls, wherever in the world they are made, wherever answered, have one thing in common: extreme brevity.

I hear her shout in the Bangalore house. 'Appa! Appa! Call from Europe!'

'Not now. I'll call later,' I say.

But I won't. When he needs me, I'm not there.

Ammu is on the couch in the living room, working her way through a book of sudoku puzzles. Between puzzles, she makes calls on her not-so-smart phone, an early model she prefers not to replace. She tries her sisters, leaves a message for Oms, and takes a good twenty minutes to tell Sarah about George's diagnosis and treatment plan. Later, she completes the puzzle she was working on, erases the numbers she had filled in with pencil, turns the page and starts a new one. Then she tries her son in Berlin. When he answers, she goes into the bedroom to tell George.

'Acha, acha, it's your son, calling from Germany.' Not strictly true. She is the one who has placed the call, but it will make George happy to think his son is calling from some faraway European country.

George is asleep in his chair, the television ear-splittingly tuned to a Malayalam news channel. He sleeps through it unhearing, unbothered by the screaming on screen between two minor party functionaries who are attacking each other's records on rape legislation. The correct phrase for George's condition, she knows, is 'deaf to the world'. There is really no point in waking him. Her son has already hung up, in a hurry to be gone without talking to his father. Perhaps this is (ever so slightly) understandable. There is no question that George is getting harder and harder to talk to. He spends much of the day in complete silence. He says nothing and hears nothing. If he does try out a few words, his voice sounds strange even to himself, a feeble croak rusty from disuse. Ammu exchanges more words – many, many more words, considering George rations out about a dozen in the course of a whole day – with the gardener Govindappa than with her own husband. When her sister and brother-in-law come to celebrate George's eighty-sixth birthday, her husband spends the entire evening sitting on an armchair with a half-smile on his face. He smiles and says, 'Ah,' when they arrive, smiles and says, 'Okay,' when they leave. And that is as far as his contribution extends.

'Get a hearing aid,' her sister tells George over cake and margaritas, correctly identifying the source of his silence. She has recognized that he is shut off from social contact, and that he likes it this way.

'What?'

'Hearing aid! Hearing aid!' Sarah gestures at her own ear, encased in a discreetly placed piece of transparent ear-shaped plastic.

'No, no, no,' George says. 'Absolutely, no! I'm not deaf.'

'Acha,' Ammu says. 'Who's saying you're deaf? You can't hear properly, that's all we're saying.'

'What?'

It makes him more stubborn. He refuses all intervention until Sarah takes them both to a hearing clinic, where an unnervingly cheerful young man in a lab coat ('He's no doctor,' whispers George) uses a machine he calls an audiometer to deliver sounds of varying loudness. The primitive contraption, attached to a pair of headphones and an array of dubiously coloured cables, has a front panel studded with mammoth frequency and decibel dials. Wearing headphones and an exasperated expression, George does what he is told, raising his hand whenever he hears an audible sound. His hand goes up only once, tentatively, before it drops. When Ammu takes the same test, her hand shoots into the air several times a minute. The difference in their hearing is made plain. George agrees to an expensive new hearing aid, controlled by his phone, with earbuds that charge on a sleek black stand. He tries it for an afternoon, for all of two hours, then takes the buds off with a decisive flourish.

'I'm not wearing them again,' he says. 'They don't fit my ears.'

'But don't you want to hear?' says Ammu.

'It's a quality-of-life question. These things reduce the quality of my one and only life. I really don't want them.'

The ridiculously expensive hearing aid is placed on a bookshelf and never used again.

Ammu wonders at his stubbornness, a quality she had failed to notice when he first appeared at her college, presenting a boiled sweet as if it held every promise of a glorious future. How had she agreed so readily? But there is another side to his stubbornness – equanimity. It is true that he has taken the cancer diagnosis without so much as a peep, taken it in his stride and got on with the business of living calmly through calamity, just as he's always done.

She leaves the phone on the bed and goes back to the couch and picks up her book of puzzles. Quickly she begins filling in numbers on a last row of unmarked three-by-three quadrants. Advanced sudoku, which she'd begun that year, needs absolute concentration. Very few numbers are shown in the large square. Deduction is called for, intuition even, an understanding of the way sudoku puzzles are set. This understanding doesn't come easy. It has to be earned by pitting yourself against the grid. There are no shortcuts. She writes in pencil and erases the numbers immediately so as to work the puzzle again and see how much faster she can solve it. The sudoku handbook says puzzle-solvers 'compete with themselves' and only with themselves. She had no idea how competitive she was until she started to work out the big grids, filling in the missing numbers. Even if she is her own sole competitor, she has to win. There is no other option. She becomes a better version of herself when she thinks about numbers and nothing else. Later, invariably soothed and rewarded, she finds it easier to face the day's problems. Numbers are clean and true. They don't change or make inexplicable decisions, unlike husbands and children whose actions are impossible to predict. Focusing on numbers reminds her of the days when she and Prasanna had followed the Hong Kong Stock Exchange, identifying and absorbing numbers as if they were nutrients, which to her mind they were and always would be, essential nutrients for a healthy life.

She hears the screen door to the bedroom slam, then the screen door to the garden. She hears splashing, George watering the flower and vegetable beds that Govindappa has already watered that morning. She thinks of going into the garden to instruct him, once again, on the perils of overwatering. But that will make him dig in his heels. She thinks of calling her son back. But what is the point? He is too distracted to talk these days, a brown man wandering around strange foreign cities, much as his parents had once done. She thinks of calling her daughter, but her daughter is busy with her own daughter, who is pregnant. Which brings up another question: when had she become a soon-to-be great-grandmother? How had it happened so quickly? How had it come to pass, considering she is still adjusting to motherhood? And her own problems, the back pain she has lately been experiencing, the trouble walking, the loss of appetite, the MRI she must take to determine the cause of her frequent falls.

Deliberately, she puts these thoughts aside. They fill her with dread, put butterflies in her chest, give her a sense of impending crisis, some new doom about to unfold. She picks up her yellow pencil and goes back to the sudoku, here at least is a country of her own, a republic of one, where she is in control and there is no darkness or chaos visible.

I'm walking the eastern edge of the district, past the site of the first anarchist squats and the neighbourhood in which the playwright Heiner Müller lived after the fall of the Wall. East and West had become one, but in his mind Müller never stopped being a citizen of East Germany. His old neighbourhood, now mine, is curiously timeless and unforgiving in the extreme. My father's diagnosis and life-changing aftermath are an irrefutable part of the forbidding streets and storefronts I pass. The drab winter-bitten faces. The shared misery.

To escape the weather, I enter the first bar I see. More downcast faces, leeched of colour and life. The music loud and speed-freak trippy, low chants over heavy bass and drums, a dirty blare of opiate-adjacent sax, familiar but hard to place.

At the bench across from me, two Americans consult notebooks.

'There must be,' says the woman. 'There's always a single German equivalent for a dozen words in English.'

'Well apparently *that* is a *frühschoppen*.'

The man gestures to a table in the centre of the room. A huddle of women in puffer jackets and ski pants.

'A crew of female shoppers?'

'Nopes. People enjoying a beer on a Sunday morning after church.'

'Obviously. Right!'

She covers her mouth and laughs chestily.

'Here's one for you,' says the man. '*Rabenmutter*, the mother raven's instinct to turn out her young.'

The woman writes it down. She says:

'Yeah, well, that's me. What about *wasserverbrauch?* Ruptured water pipe spilling on the street.'

'Actually, I can see that happening a lot in this neighbourhood.'

I approach the bar and the guy at the counter has that look, greasy hair and newsboy cap pulled sideways, pinpoint pupils, whispery strained voice out of an East Village hellpad.

'What'll you have?'

'Bourbon and the bill.'

'We have a promotion on single malt,' whispers the counterman.

'Too smoky for me. I'll take a bourbon. Large.'

'Where you from?'

'Kerala.'

'What, now?'

'It's a state. In India.'

'That's what you drink in India, bourbon?'

'Only when we run out of tiger's milk and elephant's tears.'

'Righteous.'

I'm thinking about the music. The cancer song I play on waking hasn't prepared me for the news of my father's illness. The sax keeps blaring and I ask the counter guy the name of the band and he replies shortly, as if it's the silliest question he's heard all day:

Morphine.

I swear to you that that is all it takes. I step into the avenue that reeks of heroin and walk among the faces collapsed into heroin and put my collar up against the weather that tastes of heroin and hurry towards Kotbusser Tor where the junkies gather in the afternoon. Under the station bridge, a couple of police cars. Sitting in the back of one, in heated conversation with the police, is a man who's usually on the corner. The sidewalk is clear of loiterers but for a large guy in a stained blue parka. I ask what gives. Working his nails with a pink buffer turned white in patches, he explains that someone stole a phone from the junkie in the police car. Now the usual crowd has disappeared because the police are asking too many questions.

'They'll be back soon,' he says.

I am incredulous that in Germany the police help heroin addicts find lost or stolen or bartered possessions.

'No, no, don't get the wrong idea,' says the big dealer in the parka. 'They don't care about us. They enjoy to disrupt our lives.'

'But they respect your rights.'

'They don't, man. If they respect my rights, they won't shut down my business for the whole day.'

I reply with a question I haven't asked in more than ten years:

'How much for a bag?'

We take off down the street like old friends out for a stroll, the man mountain of a dealer and his nervous foreign customer. His name is Obelix, so outlandish a name I know I won't change it if I ever write about my time in Berlin. I tell him mine and it is no less outlandish in that city. We enter a park. Under a spreading linden tree, in exchange for ten euros he hands me a small plastic bubble.

A week passes in this way. A fortnight passes. A month. How quickly heroin time flattens real time, forces each moment to collapse into itself until the metronomic tick of the clock is replaced by a smooth white hum, painless, serene, past and future melded into an endless euphoric present, free of anxiety until it's time again to score. The time lag keeps increasing until I can no longer trust my perception of hours and days. Obelix becomes my confidant, I his regular customer. As I approach Kotbusser Tor in my heavy coat and wool beanie pulled low, his big face cracks into a smile. He prepares his usual diatribe. The government, the government ... It is his great grievance. He is the loving father of three sons, but the dole gives him only three hundred euros a month. How is he expected to provide for his family on a pittance?

I say he is fortunate to receive anything at all. In my country, the government gives its citizens nothing, however many children they have. Not money. Not clean drinking water, breathable air, working roads or uninterrupted electricity. Not even a society in which the police protects citizens and criminals are put behind bars rather than in positions of power. Never mind trying to find your lost cell phone.

At the end of my speech, Obelix smiles. A cunning look enters his eyes. He says, 'Do you hope to immigrate to Germany?'

It is a question I hear often. Germans find it hard to imagine that someone from a poor country might not want to live amongst them.

'I'm a migrant,' I explain patiently, 'not an *im*migrant. In some time, in a month or two or three I'll leave.'

'But why?'

'Melanin.'

'Sorry?'

'The weather doesn't suit my melanin.'

We look up at the sky, which is cloudless and exceedingly dead. Around us, indeterminate trees gather leafless black shapes. Soundlessness. Quiet. Disquiet. Obelix nods slowly as if he's never before considered the weather as a reason to live somewhere, or to leave.

His cunning smile returns.

'Don't worry,' he says, 'you can bring your wife and kids.'

'I can't do that, my wife died.'

The smile disappears.

'No wonder. Your country reminds you of death.'

I assure him, 'We're in love with it. We welcome it like an old friend or family member. Even our movies and songs contain all the grief in the world.'

'We have in common this thing also,' says Obelix. 'Germans love death too! I'll tell you a story.'

'What kind?'

'Father–son story.'

'Oh, I don't know. Does he die of cancer?'

'No, my God.'

'Then let's hear it.'

'My father's a big man, loud and happy. He was conscripted from the village straight to the war. He came home injured, afraid of everything. As a boy I loved the idea of war. I collected helmets, uniforms, toy soldiers, a gas mask. He didn't like to see these things around the house. He was afraid.'

'Your father figured it out.'

'What?'

'Fear is prophecy.'

'So, after he came home with his visible and invisible injuries, after he changed, I decided I didn't like war after all. I put away my war games. He was not the only one who changed, the whole family changed.'

He digs for cigarettes, offers the pack, lights one when I decline.

'When the Wall fell, I was twenty-one, so excited. I left my village and went to Munich. Right away I got work on a road crew. Luckiest man in Germany, me.'

He blows smoke into the fog snagged in the trees, colourlessness upon colourlessness. Cigarette ash falls on his parka and adds to the scorches.

'When I got to Berlin, I felt I'd moved to a new country. America or Antarctica, I don't know, somewhere far. I was away from the village, I didn't fit in. Everything gave me away as an immigrant, my accent, my clothes, my obsession with money, my happiness in a large family with many children. I was a dinosaur from the days before the fall of the Wall.'

Obelix moved from the village to the city, from the European East to the European West. His nationality was the same, but his world changed. He had no allegiance to the state except as a source of subsidy.

It comes to me then, fully reasoned, logic-driven, a linear equation I've always known and never articulated. How exceptional it is to be without allegiance. Such a person can be trusted. It's the person of allegiance who must be feared.

Birthday week. I am to read from my novel at a luxury spa in the Bavarian mountains while a Berlin actor performs the German translation.

I take enough with me to taper off and quit. But I do not taper, and I do not quit. I dislike birthdays. Growing up, I was reminded that this was the day my mother had almost died. I'd be chastened and mostly alone. Now too I am alone, with a view of an unremarkable mountain the colour of old tin, ice on its slopes, peak lit by weak sunlight. The scene evokes desolation, and at one go I finish the Obelixian stash I've brought with me. All night and much of the day, I slip in and out of dreams of the dead. I see her face embedded in the ceiling cornice as she struggles to speak. I say that I want to see her again. Her reply is low and broken, 'Do more heroin.' Dead mother on the hospital bed to my left. Dead father on the bed to my right. In the middle am I, grinning. When I come to, I know this is where the dead go. To torment us in our dreams. They have nothing else to do and nowhere else to be.

The next evening, at an upstairs hall, I face a group of spa enthusiasts who have wandered in from their complex luxuries, their soft self-care regimens. From saltwater outdoor lap pools and scented hammams larger than any in Istanbul. From open fireplaces and orgone steamboats and private relaxation rooms. From Pilates, Qigong and Jivamukti classes, skiing and hiking excursions, aromatic Scandinavian or Laotian massages, classical or jazz performances at the private three-hundred-seat concert hall. From their clouds they come and fix their pale, their dissecting eyes on me.

Rabenmutter, rabenmutter, deliver me from evil.

The withdrawals hit as I begin to read. Goosebump chills on my upper arms and neck. Pre-cramps. Fire in the nerve endings. Fear in the arteries. I face a roomful of people who expect charm and intelligence from a man whose work they've never read. My reading, it goes without saying, is a shambles. Not that it matters, the actor does his job well enough. At least at the start.

Then comes the strangest question-and-answer session.

A woman wishes to say a few words. The actor, who is the mediator and translator for the evening, says she is welcome to say anything she likes. The woman's black leather jacket and sunglasses contrast fatally against the bright ski clothes of her compatriots. She rises, takes off her glasses and places them carefully on her head. Her eyes are of a translucent unsettling paleness, blue and washed out, and she speaks with the quiet authority of a college lecturer or a prosecutor at a court of law.

'German culture is a living thing,' she says, 'a golden thread that redeems Germany from Germans, a reservoir from where its people receive sustenance.' She mentions the world-encompassing spirit of Wagner, although I miss the larger point since I am hearing it second-hand. Then she asks what it is about German art that I find inspiring and if I have ever thought of moving to her country.

By now, my eyes are wet and the chills have spread like a rash. Even as I speak, I am surprised at the words that escape me, such is the distance between my mind and my body. I say I agree with her general assessment, but only when it comes to certain artists of the early twentieth century, because there were visionaries amongst them, even if their vision was of the kind that might strike one blind. I cite Leni Riefenstahl whose *Triumph of the Will* I saw at a time when I'd never been closer to disintegration. It helped me shake off the melancholy, so inhuman were the images the film set forth as inescapable truths, so pitiless were the flawless set pieces where orderly battalions merged into the architecture of the Reich. An elaborate spectacle aimed at propagating the idea that men and women were of value only if they were of value to the state. *Triumph of the Will* is a work that will hold its own in any art gallery, but only if those galleries are located near the brothel districts of certain cities, or near the central railway station along the alleys where pickpockets, prostitutes and drug dealers gather, in short, the kind of gallery that specializes in the bizarre, in sexual mania, in the appetites and fetishes that animate certain psychosexual persuasions, because the film embodies one idea and one idea only, that brutality is an aesthetic, an idea confirmed in Leni's later photographic work among the Nuba, the examination of blackness that records the exact nature of her regard for the darker races, and since the work could not have been possible without the assistance and collaboration of the leader, it was also a premonition of the world to come – and on and on I go, unsure of what

I'm saying, knowing it doesn't matter since I am incomprehensible to most of those who are staring at me, their impassive faces arranged like one face, their indifference shared like a blood type. The leather-clad woman, whose enormous sunglasses absorb what little light there is in the room – it is a wet day, already dark – says in that case Hitler was an aesthete who was self-aware enough to understand his limitations as an artist and to offer the world his frustration.

I suppress a yawn or speak through it, a yawn not of boredom but sickness. I say it's George Grosz or Otto Dix to whom Germans should refer if they wish to know how to address their own worst instincts. I cite the picture 'The Pillars of Society' from 1926 where a group of gross, or Grosz, men party into the night while the city burns around them. They are placid and sexually aroused, with daemons for brains, bright red noses, broken veins, beer slopping out of their steins. Meticulous shirt collars and double-breasted suits the colour of ash and faeces. A writer with a toilet bowl for a helmet. A man with a sword, another with a palm leaf, both instruments stained with blood. The swastika pin worn by a man in the foreground who knows the direction of the wind because he's seen a decade into the future – and here I add that as an Indian I understand swastikas even when they face the wrong way round, for there are men and women who wield the swastika for the cause of murder in my country also – and for all these reasons, I say, I am in no great hurry to move to Germany.

The actor seems reluctant to translate, and when he does, after a long pause, his version is much too short. I wonder how much he's left out. I excuse myself and wander outside. Now that the reading is over, my withdrawals have vanished and I've shakily returned to spa-enhanced wellness. I tap ash into a giant planter and gaze at the Wetterstein range, the Zugspitze looming above, those alien limestone crags that climb clumsily over untidy slopes of fir, single-mindedly reaching upward, for centuries, towards the same unattainable vastness. As I watch, I find myself deep in the sunless place from which the mountains had fallen to earth, that unmapped world at which so many generations have aimed their unspoken prayers.

Then follows my improvised birthday dinner, a lonely meal with the actor and the woman who owns the spa's bookshop. The conversation turns to the topic that seems to obsess the people I meet, particularly Germans of a certain age. The bookshop owner raises a glass of wine and makes a toast, if that's what it is.

'Once we had the luxury of *schadenfreude*, but no longer,' she says, 'now there is only *fremdscham*, shame, not for our own actions, but for the actions of others. *That* is the thing we share.' She glances in the direction of the actor and looks away. 'But among younger Germans, there's a new sensibility far removed from guilt.'

We drink. The bookstore owner mournfully butters her brot and speaks of the past. I catch a sense of aftermath. A conversation that has gone on for so long that all parties have forgotten their original thoughts and are simply repeating phrases they have said before.

She says, 'Do you know anything about the spa?'

I know as much as the next guest. That the Schloss Elmau had once been a shabby estate acquired by an evangelist, huckster and bestselling author named Johannes Müller, that princesses, countesses, heiresses, came to hear his glib ideas, for example, that music healed the wounds of war.

'He bought the spa and completed its renovation in 1916, a significant date,' she says, 'just ten years before the creation of your favourite George Grosz painting and two years after Germany had declared war on Russia. Müller's idea was to create a community of believers' – here she makes quote marks in the air – 'who told each other that Germans, and Müller in particular, had been chosen by God to wage war and create peace. Then Germany would lead the world. Perhaps this is the reason his spa is extremely popular with, ah, you know, younger people.'

The actor finishes his wine in a single draught, bangs his glass on the table and orders schnapps. He hasn't said a word all evening.

'Happy birthday to you,' says the bookshop owner.

For a moment, it seems like a real celebration. Then we are joined by the actor's fans, a section of the audience that had come only to see him. The bookshop owner becomes intensely interested in the gigantic pig's knuckle on her plate. Nobody speaks as we chew and gnaw at the tasteless meat. A poisonous silence wafts around us.

The actor's people are with him now and he comes into his own, pouring drinks, lighting cigarettes for the women. The leather trench he wears creaks when he moves, and he moves continually. A restless handsome man who rarely smiles or meets your eye. During the course of the evening, in public, he speaks English only once.

'We are too soft and we are in no mood to fight,' he says.

Judging by the expressions of those at the table, he's said something extraordinary. I catch a sense of performance, a role being enacted, the renegade who says what others are too timid to voice. He wipes the sweat from his forehead, although it is cold in the room, and says, '*Alles wird am ende gut und wenn es nicht gut wird dann ist es nich das ende.*'

When I ask, the woman to my left translates directly into my notebook. *All will be good in the end and if it is not good then it is not the end.* She shrugs, as if she has only repeated the words and has no regard for them herself. She is in her twenties, her eyes placid behind prescription glasses, and she speaks under her breath, afraid to disturb the air of anticipation that has settled in the room.

Waiters appear with more wine, more schnapps, more beer.

People hunch and speak in whispers, as if they are at church.

I use a phrase, '*Die kirche der trunkenheit.*' It sounds more itself in German: the drunken church, disciples gathered at table.

'*Zo jung kommen wir nicht mehr zusammen,*' counters the actor.

The people around the table lift their glasses. I've heard it before. But I am not young and I am glad not to be and I don't lift my glass. When the actor sees this, his expression changes. He takes a deep pull of his cigarette and extinguishes it in a saucer.

'*Ich bin stoltz ein deutscher zu sein,*' he says.

Somebody gasps.

'It is controversial,' says my neighbour.

'Controversy is a guest amongst us.'

'He said he's proud to be German.'

It is late, the room has emptied of diners but for our table. Only we and the waiters remain, elderly men in white shirts and black waistcoats, who cast glances at the clock on the wall. The bookshop owner calls for the bill, settles it, makes her excuses and leaves. Some of the young disciples get up too. Then, one by one, they leave the room until only the actor and I are left.

'*Ich bin stoltz ein deutscher zu sein,*' I say, and wait.

The actor's pale grey eyes flicker to life, but not in my direction. Now that his constituency has left, he speaks perfect English. Though his hands shake as he lifts the glass to his lips.

'Listen,' he says. 'What are you doing here?'

'I'm working. Tomorrow I'll go back to Berlin.' At that moment, I am looking forward to the frigid city, and to meeting Obelix, my only friend in the world. 'In a week I'll be on a plane out of the country. Where will you be?'

'I have no wish to go anywhere,' he says, still not looking at me, his eyes fixed on the near distance. The three-day stubble on his large stony face has been recently tended, his hair recently cut. 'I *am* where I'll be. Next week is a million miles away.'

'It really isn't.'

'Maybe I'll get married,' he says, not addressing me at all, his hands in the pockets of his tan leather coat, an expensive item, with an unbuckled belt, narrow epaulettes, and brown buttons the size of large coins. The wide lapels have deep cuts and a system of loops. Too stylish, I think, for the pressed blue jeans and fisherman's turtleneck he wears under it.

'Maybe is more certain than yes,' I suggest.

'Someone to go home to, a hot meal, clean clothes, sex you don't have to pay for,' he says. 'There's a lot to be said for marriage.'

'Not if you're the woman.'

We sit there for a while without talking, thinking our unalike thoughts, raising the glasses in our fists as if our well-being depends on it. He lights a cigarette, and his eyes never leave the frost against the window glass.

'This is my *home*,' he says in his precise way. 'Where's yours?'

'Anywhere but here,' I say, and a sense of space opens up around me. I know it is true, home is anywhere but here, and *here* applies to everywhere. Most of all, it applies to this room, this man, this conversation.

'Then I don't understand why you are here,' he says. 'Unless it's to learn from us how to be civilized.' His voice is flat, uninterested, his tone one you would use with someone met in an elevator, whom you'd never meet again. 'You don't like what I said?'

'Not much.'

'Ah, good. I say as I see.'

'You've got it all figured out.'

His gaze moves from the window then, and he fixes me with a look that he might have learned in acting school. The eyes go dead and the handsome face turns ugly. He sits erect in his seat, head tilted back in the way of patricians everywhere, and though we are the same height, he seems to be looking down at me from a superior vantage.

'You are wrong about *Triumph of the Will*. It is a triumph of art. You are wrong about Grosz, a man who changed his name so as to be less German. This is the man you hail as an expert on our culture?'

I notice his blunt hands, hard and calloused as a labourer's, his large-boned frame, the ash-blonde hair he wears in a fringe that falls into his eyes and hides his narrow forehead. He may be about thirty-five, younger than I am, and at that moment his bearing resembles a character in one of Grosz's paintings, erect and dissipated at once, a military man of the lower ranks, some *oberliutnant* or *unteroffizier*.

'I always want to know about other races,' he says. 'Us Germans are curious. All you people know is how to break things and kill yourselves.'

He drops his cigarette into his schnapps and stands. He isn't angry, but firmly removed from anger. His athlete's shoulders relax and his face empties of emotion. Only in the service of ideas or his profession does emotion come to him, and even then it comes second-hand. I sense that inside of him there is a vacuum. I can't imagine the work it takes to feel nothing.

He says: 'You destroy everything.'

The elderly waiters have put on their suit jackets and now stand by the vaulted entrance looking at us. Like the actor's youthful audience, now gone, the waiters too share a sense of anticipation. They too seem to be waiting for something to happen. One says something to the other, who nods, and both men turn away.

I am weighing what the actor has said. I am thinking it is probably true. Indians do break things. I get up to say yes, he's right, he's won our little skirmish, and he hits me in the face with the back of his hand in sight of the waiters. It rocks me back into my seat. My ears ring. The word *fremdscham* plays robotically in my head.

I take the bruise to China as a souvenir.

ALMOST CHINESE

BEIJING, SHANGHAI, 2013

The apartment I'd been allotted, on the tenth floor of an old Shanghai block, was not part of Victor Sassoon's original construction, two great buildings made in V and S shapes – to greet him with his initials when he flew into town. The original structure of seven floors had elegant apartments with high ceilings and wide views of the river. But three tenement floors had been added on top. There lived old men and women in middle-class penury. I'd step out of the elevator and see them lounging in the hallway on beach chairs. Washing hung out to dry on lines above their heads. Because they, and I, lived in small, boxlike apartments, we spent as much time as possible outside and used our boxes only to sleep. From the window, there was a view of the river (sluggish, urban, green with algae) and the city's orange skyline (toxic at all times of day or night). I was reluctant to cook because the smell stayed for days. I ate out or ordered from restaurants. I felt out of time and out of my element on a tenement floor that snaked in a giant S around the old ones readying to die.

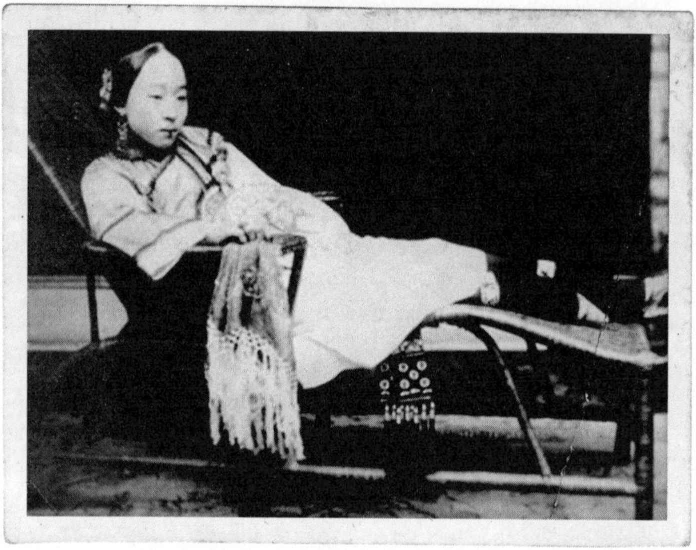

'AN INTELLECTUAL IS SOMEONE who thinks of something other than food and sex,' says Lijia. She presents me with a photograph from her collection: a Song dynasty golden lotus reclining against a bamboo chaise longue, her broken feet pointing to the past and the future. On her face is an expression of infinite nullity, all-encompassing knowledge, as if nothing can change the brute reality of what she's been through. I look at the picture and think of sex, then food.

A sprawling dusty town, Beijing hides in its old districts, in the siheyuans and hutongs, the quadrangle houses and alleyways that connect to other alleyways and courtyards. A collection of alleys is a neighbourhood. A collection of neighbourhoods is a city. This morning, Lijia's scooter passes streets that appear deserted, an unusual sight in the world's most populous city, so deserted that I wouldn't have been surprised to hear an evacuation siren warning of imminent attack, some mysterious toxic leak, citizens advised to stay indoors and not emerge until the danger has passed, and of course it won't pass. There is no hint of human activity along the narrow streets and narrower alleys, no trace presence, and as often happens to me when I find myself alone in the cities of the world, the apparent mass evacuation leaves me with a sense of deep calm as we ride sedately from one passageway to the next. The calm doesn't last very long, for soon we are in a hipster marketplace, among carefully dishevelled representatives of the international set, who drink white wine and graze above boxes of vinyl, fashion posters, T-shirts, matt music fanzines printed on the premises. BEIJING SUN THIRSTY in red neon is the building's name, and on its lowest level a field of satellite dish sunflowers are aimed at the sky. Already the serenity of the ride here seems unreal, a brief aberration.

Lijia takes a picture and makes a note of the building's name. She has a wide understanding of her city and how to present it to the world. Drawn to artefacts, without thinking of herself as a collector, she's acquired photographs, drawings, opium pipes, Qi knives and survey maps. She is most drawn to old photographic prints, because they inform the way she absorbs her surroundings and influence the way she frames her own pictures. She insists she's not a photographer as much as a documentarian, and her project is to document objects in time. Starting with a poster of a Campbell's soup can, a food item then unavailable, she records the way Western counterculture arrives in China, the way time collapses, erasing the difference between Jimi Hendrix and St Vincent. Andy Warhol and Gerhard Richter. Mahatma Gandhi and Ben Kingsley. The way everything collapses into a single capsule, *planned capitalism*, how Rightist and Leftist come to mean the opposite. Her father is a farmer and writer, her mother a painter. They are condemned as Rightists. Their class enemies, the Red Guards, are Leftists. Nothing makes sense. Each side is defined by the hat it wears. Then Deng arrives and all are unhatted.

I'm not sure what thoughts Lijia might have about her father and the defining event of her family life, considering she does not talk about those days. This much is certain: as with most stories of modern China, Lijia's origin story can be traced back to the Cultural Revolution. The sudden upending of the life she had known as a child, the chaos that ensued, unending chaos that continued for years. It must have been this that made her want to document the world around her before it collapsed once again. What better way to hold on to a moment than to take a photograph? I believe this is the secret behind what one critic has described as her 'devilishly unpredictable compositions in which household objects and human figures organize themselves according to strict if unknown laws of movement, as well as the lack thereof...'

Her father Bai, a writer of songs, poems and short stories, was deeply affected by the Cultural Revolution, as were all writers. But Bai's status of 'working-class poet' ensured that he was less affected than most. Immediately after the Revolution, the Writers' Association was suspended and its members denounced as lackeys and monsters who sided with feudalists and capitalists against the workers. Lijia's father argued that he had remained a true worker at heart even if he had been exposed to revisionist influences. Bai went as far as to join the Red Guards and denounce counter-revolutionary writers, including the head of the Writers' Association, Wang, the man who had championed Bai and brought him into the Association. This one act would change everything, but he didn't know it then. In the 1970s Bai continued to write, though not as much as before: you never knew when a sentence, a phrase, a mere couplet, might have you denounced as a counter-revolutionary. He wrote a poem, 'Absence', that was turned into a popular song in 1976 after Mao's death:

The sparrow cannot fly
In the absence of sky
The weeping willow must falter
In the absence of water
Can the revolution grow strong
In the absence of Mao Zedong?

Soon after the Cultural Revolution ended, Wang returned to the Writers' Association and engineered his long-harboured revenge. He denounced Bai as a protégé of the Gang of Four and quoted lines from 'Absence' as undeniable proof. At the subsequent conclave, there was an atmosphere of bloodlust among the writers Bai had known for most of his life. In tears, he had to plead guilty and recite long self-criticisms. He was saved once again because of his working-class reputation. But the experience broke him, and he stopped writing. He spent more and more time sitting in the lane outside the house, waving a cattail fan and smoking endless packs of Double Happiness cigarettes. His wife became the breadwinner of the family and Lijia learned early to rely upon herself.

Lijia was an only child before such a status became mandatory. The one-child policy in China has been in force more than forty years, so long that only the elderly remember a time of large families. Of course children are prized, and there are practical reasons for the love everybody showers on babies. The property goes to them, and the responsibility for looking after elderly parents. As an only child, Lijia embodies an early idea of Chinese entitlement. Her husband too is an only child, which means they're allowed to have two children.

On the ride back to Lijia's house, the streets are crowded again with schoolchildren, workers, old men and women lounging on deckchairs. It makes me long for the silence and serenity of the morning. Lijia says little as we prepare dinner. Later, as she puts her daughters to bed, I hear her tell the older one, who is in her early twenties, 'You're the selfish generation. You don't know how easy you have it, how much your parents and grandparents had to work for you to live the easy life. You get all the attention and money without being grateful. Do you deserve it?'

NOT ALL TWENTY-YEAR-OLDS FEEL they've been lucky in life. Greg, a photographer I knew from my days with *Asiaweek* in Hong Kong, has been showing me around Shanghai. One afternoon he says, 'I know a man, we call him *the sound guy* because he's done the music for some of Eric's movies. He's hosting a vinyl listening party. It's an outstandingly typical Shanghai scene, you should come.'

Held in a nuclear bunker that has been turned into a nightclub, music bouncing angularly off the concrete walls, I am introduced to George Ziang, a small man in his mid-twenties, square-faced and mild, with a shock of boyish hair falling across his forehead. Later that week, we meet for lunch at a restaurant. He gestures at the dish of fish livers and recommends it with enthusiasm because each spoonful represents several dead fish.

'Eight fishes died for this delicious morsel,' he says, swallowing a spoonful of minuscule livers.

I try a small taste, even if I'm unable to summon much enthusiasm. The livers slither into my throat like a school of tiny fishes. I have to wash them down with a few large shots of baijiu. The banquet has been served in a private room on the top floor of a restaurant where the staff seems to know George well. There are repeated enquiries after the health of his father, a businessman famous for his construction projects. I mention Lijia's idea of the selfish generation and ask if George too thinks it's a good time to be young in China.

'Not for all of us,' he says. 'It's true for women more than men, especially in Shanghai. It's no good being a man in this town, not any more. In Shanghai, a girl won't marry you if you're renting. You have to own a place and put it in her name too. No property, no marriage. When you go to a club, the first thing they say is, "Hello, what job do you do? Where do you live?"

'I met someone at the agency where I work. I design sound for ad movies. We used to stay late because the deadlines were impossible. We'd order in, fast food mostly. She became my girlfriend. Then one day she tells me she's also seeing a British guy, a journalist, and when he's in town she'll be shacking up with him. He knows about me, I know about him. She wants his baby because it'll be Eurasian. She told me, "I want his seed." Just like that. She's thirty-four and she wants a baby before she turns thirty-five. I met the journalist. We exchanged notes and all that. I asked him what he liked about her. He said, "Ruthless practicality and heart. She's got heart."

'I told him that in simplified Chinese they dropped the heart symbol from the character for *love*. How can you love without heart? Unless you don't believe in love. That's the plain truth of it. We don't believe in love. Or God. We believe in money. Before we gamble, we pray. If we want a son, we pray. At our Buddhist temples, we pay to pray. Why is the statue of the Buddha gold-plated? The more we pay, the more Buddha takes care of us.'

YUAN YUAN LIKES THE SOUND OF HER NAME. The name of money said twice, once for luck, once again for more luck. She likes the sound of her official status, *liudong renkou*. She likes to think of herself as part of the floating pop, a migrant worker, because everybody is *liudong renkou* whether they know it or not. In her first week in the city, she works as a cigarette girl, walking around with a tray of cigarettes and a smile on her face. Soon enough, the smile is gone. The money is erratic and the work bores her to tears. Literally: she cries at odd moments. She asks around the local clubs and restaurants and finds work as a singsong girl at a multilevel dim sum place on Nanjing Road. But she started singing too late in her life. Her voice isn't trained and it shows. Even when the customers are drunk, they aren't drunk enough to overlook her lack of finesse. She embarrasses herself to such an extent that she begins to dread the day. She can't go on. She quits the job and starts work as a model.

'Easiest job ever,' she says. 'Even if you're bald and fat, you get assignments. And as you can see, I'm not bald or fat. But I got tired of it soon enough. My mother was a leader of the Young Pioneers, like communist Girl Scouts. She gave speeches at school occasions and waved the flag at important ceremonies. For most of her life she worked at a secret military factory, safeguarding our country's future. She told me I should aim higher in life.'

Yuan Yuan orders yogurt and asks the waiter to bring American cigarettes.

'My new job is the best job I've had. I'm an English teacher, meaning I stand around doing sweet fuck-all and they give me two hundred an hour. Seriously, to do absolutely nothing. But it's not a nine-to-five job, more like nine-to-nine. The students call you up at any time of day or night, with some crazy stupid question. "Hey, how you pronounce *cough* in English? How come *slough* pronounced different?" What can you say? I tell them, don't expect English to make sense. You just got to learn it.

'I tell my students they're too old for Simon Says, but they love it. I never say "Simon says". Simon can go to hell. Simon can fuck himself. *I* say "Yuan Yuan says". If I say "jump" and they jump, they're disqualified. If I say "Yuan Yuan says jump, Yuan Yuan says fly", then, yeah, they better jump and fly.'

She takes a pocket mirror out of a small sequinned purse and checks her eye make-up. With an eyebrow pencil: a quick touch-up, expertly performed.

'I'm tired of this place. Let's go somewhere. You decide.'

'The Apartment?'

'It's a meat market. Expat guys and Chinese girls. Oh wait, that's all of Shanghai. By the way, I like your black eye.'

Her smile is dazzling, teeth large and white, gums pink. Her eyes are blue, eyelashes caked with mascara. She strokes and pets her long hair, which is platinum blonde and starlet wavy. The floral V-neck midi dress is from Cos, the velvet platform slip-ons from Shanghai Tang.

'Nice ring, are you married?'

'No. Are you?'

She eats her yogurt and smokes her Winston.

'I'm looking for a husband for one night.'

HER EYES WIDEN WHEN I SAY I'M A WRITER. A bray issues. Briefly, she covers her mouth with a pale, plump hand and sits low in the plastic chair, legs planted to the ground. On a pair of heavy, black-rimmed spectacles, her untidy eyebrows are never at rest. She's come directly from the office, carrying numerous shopping bags, a backpack, a fringed leather purse styled like a saddlebag. Her name is Sabrina.

'Writer. What you write?'

'Books.'

'That mean you poor! You poor *and* you thief.'

'But how am I a thief, Sabrina?'

'You steal people, you take their words and appearance and then you put in story, am I right?'

I note her agitated eyebrows. 'Right.'

'Mainly, writer means poor!'

The plump hand covers the mouth: the low-pitched bray issues.

That year, China's economy boasts the fastest rate of growth in the world. Every citizen is part of the glorious machine. Writers too, but only if they write bestsellers. In the Chinese scheme, a poet or novelist is unquestionably poor. Sabrina has rapidly and accurately assessed my financial prospects, or lack thereof.

'How come you have black eye?

'I picked it up in Germany.'

'Where you from?'

'India.'

'Really. You are from Indian? You not look. You handsome, almost like Chinese.'

This is the great compliment. To be almost as handsome or pretty as a Chinese. Like capitalism, racism in China is a socialist enterprise apportioned equally against anyone who isn't Chinese. Sabrina is a shining example of the genre.

'I never had dinner with Indian before. Normally I don't like Indian.'

'I'm your first Indian?'

'Yes,' she says. 'Yes!' She laughs and forgets to cover her face. The teeth are on display, unevenly crowded into her thin, pursed mouth. Lips bitten bloody, missing strips of skin.

It is our first meeting following a brief conversation on a dating app.

When I ask if she'd like a drink, she says she'd rather skip the drinks and go straight to dim sum. We order xiao long bao. I am sucking carefully at the soup inside the dumpling when she asks her question.

'Why Indians keep slaves?'

The dumpling falls inelegantly into the bowl. Some of the soup spills on my shirt. She hands me a napkin.

'We don't keep slaves.'

'Everybody know Indian keep slaves. The whole family works for you for life on minimum wage because of caste. Right?'

I've never thought about Indian domestic servants in this way. In the poorest regions of the country, workers are bonded for generations. The entire family is owned. In the cities, even if domestic work brings no pension or health insurance or job security, life is less dire. Work is plentiful even when it's demeaning. At the city restaurant of the moment, the extended family is on one table, eating and drinking, and on a separate table sits the maid, who has been offered nothing, not a sip or a morsel. Her job is to keep an eye on the children. Later, in the kitchen at home, she will have her meal, inexpensively. In that sense, I've had slaves all my life. Kept by my parents and later by me. To clean the floors and toilets, to sweep and mop and dust for a pittance, who never sit at the same table even if they've been with the family for years. I'm thinking of Sangita, a woman who worked for me when I lived in Bombay, whose last name had never been offered. It would have been a way of making plain her caste. After two or three years of cleaning house and mopping floors and washing clothes, my obliviousness about her caste must have rankled. She asked for a holiday on Ambedkar's birthday, and said, just like Jesus is your God, Ambedkar is our God. I said something flippant about praying to a man in a blue suit. Why not? she said. You pray to a naked man nailed to a cross.

It was Sangita's lesson for me.

All you people know is how to break things and kill yourselves.

'Right,' I tell Sabrina, ashamed.

'POURQUOI AVEC SON PÈRE?'

PARIS, 1988 | COCHIN, 1975 | PARIS, 1988

After much expense and effort, he managed to acquire a bidet that had been custom-made in Paris and shipped to Cochin. As soon as it was installed, a day-long procedure, a steady procession of neighbours came over to have a look. It was the only bidet in Cochin, possibly in the whole of South India, and it became the talk of the town. His wife's objections were manifold, and they were overruled. Over the years, bidets were installed in every bathroom in the house.

AFTER DARK, THE POOR EMERGE. Small crowds on the boulevards, smoking our last cigarettes and drinking from bottles carried openly and legally. Cobalt night presses in from all sides. In the air, a smell of roast meat and woodsmoke, the kind of smell that drives the destitute to crime. We know each other by sight and go about our business, circumscribed by day and resurrected after sunset. I've been sleeping at a bookshop, in a room full of rare volumes. I ran out of money in my second week in the city. As a migrant from a country with limits on foreign exchange, I don't have a credit card. But coffee is available at the bookshop, and once a day I eat crêpes from a street stall on Rue de la Huchette.

On Sunday morning, I take a train from Les Halles to the Hare Krishna temple at Sarcelles on the city's outskirts. The Hare Krishnas provide free meals, pure vegetarian only, and allow you to take with you when you leave a few pieces of bruised fruit or a roll. The temple stands on a residential street behind a green wire fence that has broken through in parts. White plastic chairs under a tin roof. Makeshift tables. Throwaway cutlery. A house in disrepair. About a dozen of us come for the food, and the Hare Krishnas who serve us do so sullenly. But we eat our fill and return each Sunday.

I spend much of my time walking around. Or I sit at the scarred communal table on the first floor and try my hand at translations from Baudelaire and Rimbaud and Verlaine. I come to understand that it's difficult to work when you're hungry. Hunger dims your vision and interferes with your judgement. You think you're on the verge of rapture but it's only anxiety, and all it brings is your unravelling. But I have the good fortune, I believe at the time, to meet a young English thief who teaches me how to live off the land.

'They fat, we thin,' he says, indicating the good citizens walking past the bookshop on Rue de la Boucherie. 'Our job is to take, theirs to give.'

His name is as extraordinary as his appearance. Gary Gilmore. Recognizable in a crowd by the white-blonde hair and friendly sneer. He says he isn't related to the American thief and murderer whose last words were 'Let's Do It' (a slogan later appropriated by an athletic shoe company). When I ask why he's never changed his name, he says he enjoys the association with a true criminal legend.

'Where are we, Paris?' he says.

'That's what they're saying.'

'Actually, I've been here two years. I've never had a job, and I've never been hungry, not once, not really.'

'Well, how do you manage?'

'I'm a thief, is what, but I only steal one item.'

'A specialist.'

'Alcohol from the supermarkets in the suburbs, the farther out the better. City ones don't work. Too suspicious.'

'You steal alcohol.'

'And sell it to bar owners on the Left Bank.'

He flexes his hands and grins.

'What do you say to that?'

'It's one way to make a living.'

'And doesn't it make some mad sense that I share my name with a famous criminal?'

'Gary Gilmore, pleasure to meet you.'

'Want to come along next time?'

I hesitate only a moment. It leads, inevitably, to arrest. But that isn't the point of this story. This story is about Baudelaire's grave, the reason I've come to Paris in the first place. Why Baudelaire? I'll explain.

In September 1975, we visited my mother's oldest brother in Cochin. My family had returned from New York to Hong Kong, and once a year we went to South India to 'keep in touch with our heritage' as my father liked to put it. I remember my first meeting with the man whom I in private called Baudelaire Uncle. He shook hands formally and was kind, which I wasn't expecting. In the family, they spoke fearfully of his rudeness and brilliance. For most of his adult life he'd been working on a Malayalam translation of *Les Fleurs du Mal*. But this wasn't the only reason they considered him odd. He wrote a book and published it, a fantastical accomplishment in that backwater town. They didn't know, and I'd find out only later, that the book was a torment to him. His sole publication. An obscure legal tome titled *Public Law: Some Aspects* that got him invited to lawyers' conferences he had no wish to attend. I asked once if I could see a copy and it was as if I'd said something dreadful. There were hundreds of books in his library but no copies of his own. He couldn't bear to look at it because it reminded him that his dream of becoming a writer had come to nothing more than a slim book on jurisprudence. Sixteen years later, at the British Library, I found a copy that had never been borrowed and made a note of the opening paragraph of the opening chapter, 'The Inarticulate Major Premise of Modern Public Law':

> *History to a great extent supports the view that forms of government proceed in a circle. Monarchy degenerates into tyranny and is overthrown. Aristocracy that comes in its stead degenerates into an oligarchy. It is pushed out by the people for establishing what Aristotle calls a constitutional government (but which in modern political terminology will be called a democracy) which degenerates into what Aristotle calls democracy (but which we may call a mobocracy) which is displaced by a dictatorship which is nothing but a monarchy in the sense of a rule by one man. The cycle then will continue.*

Of his other writing, I knew only that a literary journal in the UK had published an essay or story titled 'Inside Baudelaire'. He had had no luck finding a publisher, had written no more essays or fiction, had continued with his translations in the hope of publishing a collection. In my eyes he was a poète manqué, a lawyer whose secret life was poetry. Like my father, whose ambition was to write a novel. But I understood all this much later. That day in Cochin, I went into his library during the siesta hour. The room took up the entire front wing of the tile-roofed tharavad, and all four walls were lined with books and each title was by or about Baudelaire, in French or in English translation. Above the desk were three portraits, the poet as a handsome young dandy, as a slightly older man, still charming, still stylish, and the famous late image of a haunted syphilitic. In the sunlit bathroom off the library, I found a bidet.

After tea, it was time to go visiting and my uncle put me in the passenger seat. The vehicle was a legend for its extravagance. A green 1957 Morris, thrillingly inappropriate for rural Cochin and its narrow mud lanes. The wide leather seats and dashboard of dark wood struck me as components in a dream of another life, in which we were a distinguished family setting off for an evening of repose.

'A.T. Markose, sir,' said a grinning neighbour as we backed out.

'We're going to Always,' my uncle said.

It was his joke for the suburb of Alwaye: once you get to Always, it's difficult to leave.

He drove past the city centre, and they came out of their houses to stare at the legend on the bonnet, Oxford, its spacious cursive embedded above the enormous grille – and at him. Pencil moustache freshly shaped, he wore sunglasses and a short-sleeved cream tunic he called a bush shirt. There were numerous pleated pockets. There was a suggestion of epaulettes. His seat was pushed all the way back. The car picked up speed on the highway and left other vehicles behind. I remember the sound of the engine, soft and loud at the same time, and the black speed dial with its white markings, like a big clock, and the way the indicator stayed steady at fifty-five for most of the drive. We passed deserted village squares and endless waterways where men poled narrow, standing canoes. Then we turned into a side lane and parked. Markose would not enter the house, a chore he left to Ammu and his wife. He set off with his hands behind his back, nodding at me to come along. We took a path that curled through the village, past emerald paddies turning purple in the dusk.

He had questions for me, accompanied sometimes by answers.

A stampede of elephants kills twenty-four people in Orissa. And do you know what the newspapers report? I did not. Most ignore the stampede but not a single one misses the big news of the day, the Tamil movie star MGR is about to form a political party. Why do you think, said Markose, Indians care more about the movies than about the deaths of their countrymen? With a teenager's certainty I said it was because life was not worth living, for Indians, much less preserving, why bother when it was so brief and the next life would almost certainly be better? People should be allowed to die if death was in their stars. It isn't our place to interfere in the natural order of things. And, I said, the dead return to us soon enough. The answer must have pleased him. He nodded as if I'd said something thoughtful, though I had not. He said in time I'd discover that the dead did not return. Their peculiarities fade first, then their faces and last of all their voices. In time, he said, you'll find that our forgetfulness about death and a hundred other things, for example, the keeping of slaves, the contempt for people of darker races and castes, the belief in godmen, the denial of equality, fraternity and liberty, all this is not the sole prerogative of Indians.

Then, as if everything he had said was a prelude to his real subject, he turned to the poet whose book, in his opinion, announced the arrival of modernity into the world, whose opinions were simultaneously outmoded and avant-garde, whose insights were like points of light at a planetarium where an artificial sky boasted a hundred, no, a thousand electric stars. Here was a man whose reckless lifestyle brought him syphilis in his late teens or early twenties, who discovered that desire and its consequences went hand in hand, thanks to the disease for which there was no cure. Even a skeletal biography told of tragedy amid the consolations of poetry.

'To read Baudelaire is to gather up the world and bring it inside.'

'What do you feel, inside?'

'There is no inside,' said Markose.

After I grew familiar with the poet's work, I wondered if it was this that so fascinated my uncle. When he entered those visions of voyages and damnation, tender giantesses, horror, voluptuousness, he no longer felt the contours of his own life. He became as one with the writer he admired.

I believe there were affinities. Illness might have been one – Baudelaire Uncle had had problems with his heart – but also there was the restless intellect and the vast private unhappiness I sensed, of which Markose never spoke. He had a way of clenching his jaw, which gave his face the cast of an eagle or a falcon. At those moments he seemed fearsome, and I was happy I wasn't the cause of his distress.

The main object of his ire was Baudelaire's stepfather. Even now, the name Jacques Aupick recalls to me Markose's revulsion, which I might have acquired second-hand. He said there was nothing filial about the poet's feelings for his mother. His relationships with women were a way to exact revenge against Caroline, who had abandoned him, whom he had to beg for money, who judged and misjudged him, who had remarried when her son was but five and chosen a military man of all men, a soldier with no feeling for the arts or for the extraordinary stepson he was privileged to raise. The poet only slept with those women who took his money and betrayed him, said Markose. And this too he desired. The revenge of degradation.

For Jeanne Duvall my uncle reserved only sympathy.

'Imagine how Europe must have been at the time,' he said. 'What she must have had to endure. The woman lodged in the heart of the French Empire's greatest poet. Jeanne was one of us. And by that, I mean a woman of Africa or Asia who marked a part of Europe as hers. Imagine her surrounded by men and women who saw her only as colour, a piece of sun-dried driftwood from the colonies.'

He took a small pipe out of his pocket and filled it with tobacco from a pouch. He lit two matches at once and stroked the bowl with the flame. I'd never seen him smoke before.

'Only one man knew her solitude was the state of true innocence.'

'The poet who loved her.'

'Yes,' said Markose. 'Yes, the poet who loved her solitude.'

He stopped walking. In a soft and distant voice, he said:

'Like Jeanne, Indians are the detritus of Empire, and it is our duty to use its tools to dismantle it.'

'It's raining ... Which tools do you mean?'

'The language we're speaking, first of all, and in my case the study of law and the reading and translation of French, which is the language of culture. More so than English. Do you see?'

This was how he talked. Anniethottam Thomas Markose: Baudelaire Uncle. I set down here those things I understood at the time. On what became our first and last walk the summer I turned fourteen, he asked what it was like to be a migrant in a place like Hong Kong. Was it unbearable? It was the first time I'd thought of myself in that way, and I had no reply. Now I'd say it's a question I'm unqualified to answer. I've always been a migrant. He mentioned his disappointment at Baudelaire's grave in Cimetière du Montparnasse. But he said nothing more as we passed the ill-lit dwellings along the main road of Alwaye and began the trek back to the house where a family waited in the rain. Before we entered, he emptied out the pipe, wrapped it in a handkerchief and placed it in the pocket of his pleated trousers. 'Later,' he said. I thought, yes, later I'll ask the important questions. Why was he translating *Les Fleurs du Mal*, something no single translator had attempted? And why into Malayalam? But I never got the chance. He was struck down by a heart attack at a legal conference in London, his Baudelaire translation incomplete, unpublished, unknown.

After the shock of Markose's death, books arrived from his library in Cochin. A gift from his daughters. Milton's *Comus: A Masque* published by Routledge in 1906, the frontispiece an engraving of a young man playing a pipe in a meadow, his hunting horn on the ground beside him, and a caption, THE SOOTHEST SHEPHERD THAT ERE PIP'T ON PLAINS. *Baudelaire as a Literary Critic*, published in 1964, and F.W. Leakey's *Baudelaire and Nature*, 1969, both addressed to me in my cousin's hand. *Sister Beatrice, and Ardiane & Barbe Bleue*, a cloth-covered pocket edition in sea-green (in fact, the exact green of Markose's 1957 Morris) of two plays by Maurice Maeterlinck, translated from the French into English verse and published at Ruskin House, London, in May 1924. I examined the last book first. Tucked between the Bluebeard play and the endpaper were four sheets held in place with a bit of tape. The first was a translation from the English of 'Epilogue' with the Malayalam written between and around the lines. The other pages, taken from a child's exercise book, were filled with my uncle's lawyerly shorthand. I made a code. The 'm' and 'r' and 'n' were alike, a series of short strokes, and it was the same with the 'l' and 'i' and 't'. Like my father, he used a mixture of Malayalam and English when writing quickly, his pen racing to keep up with his thoughts. In this way I recovered the abandoned draft of a novel or short story, 'Inside Baudelaire'.

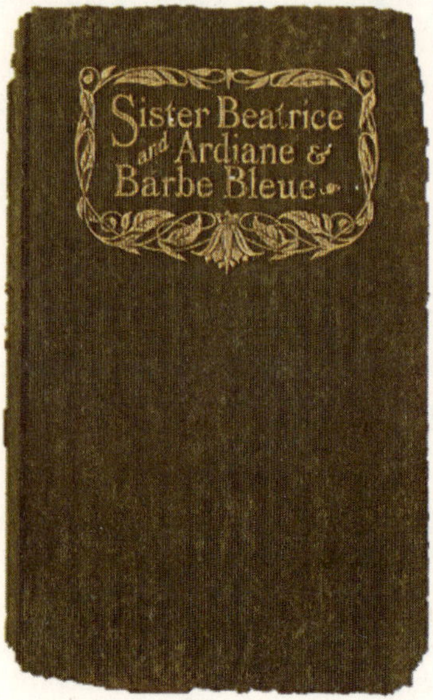

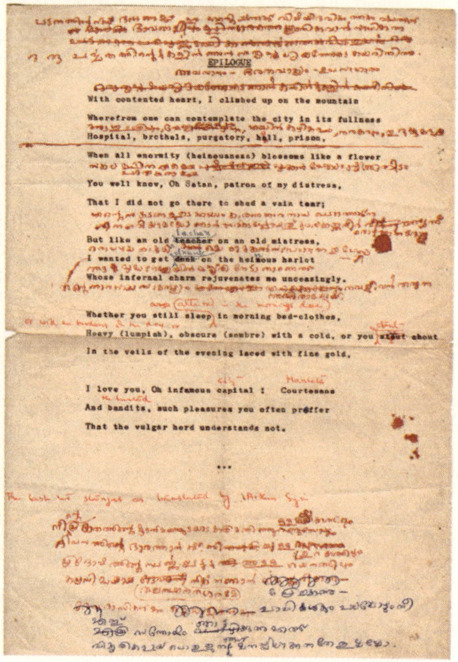
EPILOGUE

With contented heart, I climbed up on the mountain

Wherefrom one can contemplate the city in its fullness
Hospital, brothels, purgatory, hell, prison,

When all enormity (heinousness) blossoms like a flower

You well know, Oh Satan, patron of my distress,

That I did not go there to shed a vain tear;

But like an old teacher on an old mistress,
I wanted to get drunk on the heinous harlot
Whose infernal charm rejuvenates me unceasingly.

Whether you still sleep in morning bed-clothes,
Heavy (lumpish), obscure (sombre) with a cold, or you strut about
In the veils of the evening laced with fine gold,

I love you, Oh infamous capital ! Courtesans
And bandits, such pleasures you often proffer
That the vulgar herd understands not.

...

The PORT OF BORDEAUX SMELLS OF SAWDUST, pitch, woodsmoke and fear. It is second only to Nantes in the number of slaves it has shipped to the New World, and second to none in the wealth it has acquired from the abduction and enslavement of men, women and children. The date is 9 June 1841, seven years before the French slave trade is officially abolished. A light rain washes the filthy paving stones of the quay. The *Southern Skies* is at port. Provisions are loaded amid grunts and shouted orders: salted meats, casks of wine, tobacco, coffee, gunpowder. A twenty-year-old poet embarks, carrying two bags and a porcelain-topped walking stick. He wears a new frock coat and a look of supreme boredom. The gangway heaves as violently as his stomach. It's late morning by the time the halyards are hoisted and the *Southern Skies* sets sail for Calcutta. The ship leaves port as if it were just another journey, as if there were no special passenger on board. What if the poet had given himself up to the fate his stepfather had plotted? What if he hadn't jumped ship at Mauritius, the *Southern Skies'* first port of call, and had landed in Calcutta as planned? It's safe to say he never would return. He'd vanish into the fleshpots of the city, there to drink or drug himself to death. Calcutta would have altered the course of European literature and delayed, if not aborted, the birth of modernism.

From this speculation, Markose imagines a morning in the poet's life. Everything has left his head but an image. Not Jeanne, but a beggarwoman glimpsed on the street. Her skin is pale and dirty, her hair red. He can think of nothing else. Memories are leaving him one loved word at a time, until at the end nothing will be left but *crenom – Sacre Nom* melded into gibberish. 'I imagine God, bored, devising for you a special punishment,' wrote Markose, 'as he would punish a composer with deafness, or a dancer with arthritis. A poet reduced to two syllables!'

Now Markose describes his hero's first glimpse of Jeanne Duvall. She walks onstage in a maid's outfit to say her only line of the night. *Madame le thé est servie.* Abundant hair of a type he has never seen. Skin of a hue he cannot imagine. The poet forgets that he has come to meet the actress who plays Jeanne's madame. He rushes to the florist for a bouquet and leaves it by the stage door with her name on a card. A *scandâle* that Baudelaire ignored the ingénue he was courting for a mulatto of no consequence, who will decimate his health and reduce his fortune. 'That maligned woman,' wrote Markose. 'Far from home, never more than a step from destitution.' Then, a sudden tirade against Angela Carter, of all people, whose story 'Black Venus' (Markose wrote) portrays Jeanne as a figure of sloth, derides *the custard apple of her stinking Eden,* her *native indolence,* in a *vegetable trance* for hours, for days. *She wouldn't have known what knowledge was for, would she?* Lowest, unkindest, maddest cut of all, Angela Carter imagines the poet speaking to his mulatto in words he wouldn't have uttered in any language.

> *Baby, baby, let me take you back where you belong, back to your lovely, lazy island where the jewelled parrot rocks on the enamel tree and you can crunch sugar cane between your strong, white teeth, like you did when you were little, baby. When we get there, among the lilting palm trees, under the purple flowers, I'll love you to death ... My monkey, my pussycat, my pet...*

And the chapter ends as it begins. An imagined day in the life of the poet. Nothing to show for a morning of work but a four-line stanza. How easy to lose heart (wrote Markose) and how miraculous that we do not, that I can hear you now across a century's ennui:

Blanche fille aux cheveux roux,
Dont la robe par ces trous
Laisse voir la pauvreté
Et la beauté

My first visit to Cimetière du Montparnasse follows a family trip to London for the wedding of Baudelaire Uncle's daughter. From London, against my parents' wishes, I fly to Paris and spend the night in a waiting room at the Gare du Nord, a thin Kashmiri shawl around my shoulders. I have 400 francs. A duffel bag with some toiletries and a camera. A pigskin hipflask with a hinged stainless-steel cap. A pair of black trousers with a velvet stripe on the sides. Some white shirts with billowing bishop sleeves (even then, even without money, I must have had a dandy's sense of style, of which my uncle would have approved). And a volume of *Les Fleurs du Mal.*

One afternoon, I spot a bookshop on the Left Bank with an interesting name, and wander in to browse. I find a new edition of *The Thief's Journal* and consider slipping it into my pocket. But the bookshop is family-owned, clearly independent, and now that I am no longer in my teens, I seem to have acquired an ethical sense. Abruptly, a wild-haired old man approaches, a cat in his arms. 'Are you Dravidian?' he asks. I am surprised enough to reply in the affirmative. He has that look, some scholarly hobo, whereas the cat, a calico, is perfectly groomed. Small and rumpled and birdlike, the man's attention seems drawn to a hundred things at once. But the cat looks me straight in the eye. 'Do you need a place to stay,' the old man asks. 'Yes,' I say to the calico, 'yes.'

And that is how I move into Shakespeare & Co.

I spend the night among great piles of books. Untidy stacks on every surface. Even the damp toilet is lined with them. The first floor has a writing room with a large square table and single beds secreted against the walls. The window opens upon a courtyard. At night, the beds are pulled out and the floors are crowded with sleeping bags. In the day, personal belongings are hidden away in recesses and alcoves. There is no shower. On Wednesdays, a group of us go to the municipal baths. Shut from Sunday to Tuesday, there is always an unwashed crowd waiting at the entrance on Wednesday morning. The shower is a roomy cubicle. You push a steel button to start the water. It flows for a few minutes and stops and then you hit the button again as you soap yourself.

Located across the bridge from the terrifying pontefract of the Notre Dame, the bookshop has already become a tourist spot. Its residents are post-hippies or early backpackers. George calls them tumbleweeds. George Whitman is the old man's name, and he owns the bookshop. Once, he too had been a tumbleweed who travelled to various corners of the globe, including India. He'd been treated with such hospitality that he felt it was his duty to return the favour. Head tumbleweed is Tim, a bearded American in his early thirties. He wears crumpled denim shirts and torn blue jeans, and his battered Adidas boasts a hole from where his big toe protrudes. But there is an Amex card in his back pocket for the meals to which he treats himself at the café around the corner. One night, dining on roasted peanuts, I see him enjoying a dish of crème brulée. I've filled my hip flask with pastis bought at the corner store. I take a sip and watch as a waiter in a spotless white apron refills Tim's glass of wine.

I am not envious, not really. I've been working all day. Only the poem is real to me as it unfolds over an AABB rhyme and short lines. It takes two days to make the first stanza, and though I can't hope to reproduce the syllabics, I am happy with the rhymes. If I knew the language, I would have translated the poem into Malayalam. I'd have continued my uncle's work and finished his book of translations. But I have no Malayalam, I have only this:

Pale girl with the flame-red hair,
The holes in your dress lay bare
The shape of your poverty
And beauty

Gary Gilmore and I embark on the first of our ventures to the supermarkets on the outskirts. We each slip bottles of cognac and whisky into our trousers, two bottles apiece. Outside, the bottles go into carrier bags Gary has thoughtfully brought along. We go into another supermarket, and so on, until we have around two dozen bottles, and enough money between us to finance a few days of drinking and eating. When Gary hears I play the guitar, he borrows one from a friend and we work the metro from the Louvre to Les Halles. The seven stations of the busker's cross. Unlike the other buskers, who keep office hours, Gary and I work an hour or two at the most. We share the money evenly. I am the musician, but it is Gary who goes up to the commuters and says, '*Quelque-chose pour le musique, s'il vous plait,*' and waits, intimidatingly, until he is given a few coins.

One night, penniless, I visit a supermarket at Les Halles which the street people call the free market. I take a bottle of whisky out of its case and secrete it and walk to the bookstore. Two nights later, I try again with the same brand of whisky. When I leave the store, they are waiting. At the commissariat, the detectives ask what I do for a living.

'*Écrivain,*' I say.

They laugh.

'*Vous a volé vendre ou boire?*'

'*Boire,*' I say indignantly, for it is true.

They leave me in a cell with a man who is naked but for a pair of horn rims. Civil and soft-spoken, he will not stop whispering in a language I cannot understand. The policemen return and tell me to leave my spectacles with them and fetch my passport. They check my visa and let me go. In their manner, I sense respect. Unlike the Hare Krishnas, the police don't treat the poor as if we are not quite human.

I know my time in Paris is nearing its end and I can no longer put off my visit to Montparnasse's quiet city, where I wander for an hour looking for the gravesite. I expect a mausoleum or modest tomb. Even the dictator Porfirio Díaz has rated a grand memorial. I wander, lost, until a man who is tending the flowers gives me directions. I locate it at last, as Markose had before me. Decrepit, uncared for, littered with cigarette butts, dead flowers, empty bottles, handwritten notes, foodstuff, unnameable junk. The poet is buried with his mother and stepfather in a grave so narrow they would have been stacked one on top of the other. Nearby, scrawled red graffito: *Pourquoi avec son père?* But it isn't the right question.

'*Il est pas son père,*' I said, '*il est son beau père. Pourquoi avec son beau père?*'

STILL LIFE WITH SPACESHIPS,
OR,
HOW TO LEAVE A HUSBAND

DELHI, 2017 | ALGECIRAS-TANGIER, 2019 |
MUI NE, 2020

Unlike the footnote, the Remarkable Rhetorical Device is not relegated to the back of the book. Unlike the headnote, it does not seek to elucidate but to mystify and delight.

HOTEL
JANPATH
NEW DELHI
INDIA

IT'S A FAMILY SAYING: DON'T GO NORTH. She goes, of course, and stays for years. At first, she checks into a cheap hotel in Connaught Place. It is summer and she learns to go out early in the day or late in the evening. The afternoons are so hot she stays in her room with the air conditioner blasting. Her freelance job with a travel magazine consists of writing articles headlined 'Weekend Retreats from Delhi' or 'Delhi: 12 Historical Walks' or 'Delhi's Beloved Neighbourhoods.' Whenever someone says how inhospitable Delhi is, how hot, how cold, how indifferent, how difficult, she experiences the balm of satisfaction. She likes the extreme seasons, the dangers lurking in broadest daylight, the dumbfounded silence when she says her name. They always ask her to say it again.

'Chachiamma Jacob.'

'What kind of name is that?'

'Chachiamma is my grandmother's name.'

'You are from?'

'She was from Kerala. I'm from all over the place.'

All they clock is *Kerala*. So remote, that any kind of strangeness makes sense. She feels the same about Delhi. How unlikely it is that anyone would live here. When she and her girlfriend drive to Gurgaon, Haryana, it becomes all too clear. The state appears in headlines about murders, gang rapes, institutionalized corruption. There are shootouts on the main road between police and gangsters. Usually, the gangsters win. They drive past endless fields that fizz electric in the dark. A hairy darkness of heat amid the smell of raw earth. A mall looms up out of the night, blazingly lit, foreign as a spaceship. Priya, who is driving, gasps, and the car fishtails for a second. The entire construction or suburb or city-state is like this, deserted rural landscapes broken up by spaceships. They hold hands and drive in silence with the windows up, expecting the worst.

On the way home, they are stuck behind a couple on a two-wheeler. The pillion rider clutches a toaster oven to her side, the plug falling free. Her long hair, under an unbuckled helmet, flies into the face of the man who is driving too fast, the woman barely hanging on. They seem precarious, on the verge of disaster.

'That could be us,' says Priya.

'Yeah, that could never be us.'

'Why not? She could be me, a couple of years down the line, hanging on for dear life to a kitchen implement.'

'If that couple is us, you're the man. You're driving?'

'I may drive the car, but you drive me.'

'I drive you. To what?'

'To drink,' says Priya, rolling her eyes.' To distraction. I don't know what else.'

'Watch out for the camel cart.'

That year, Gurgaon changes its name to Gurugram, in keeping with the ungodly godliness of the new dispensation.

'The history of the capital is right there, Pri,' Chachiamma says. 'Changing names overnight. Kingsway Road is Rajpath. Queensway is Janpath. Curzon Road becomes Kasturba Gandhi Marg. Race Course Road is Lok Kalyan Marg. Connaught Place is Rajiv Chowk. Where will it end? Pretty soon I'll have to change my name from Jacob to Jai Kumar.'

All she has is an address, or half an address. Block C, Safdarjung Enclave, ask for Harinder. It happens to be fifteen minutes from the airport. The old Sardar who lives there, she's been told, is in the early stages of dementia.

'Over my dead body,' he says, when she asks to look at the apartment on the first floor. He shuts his eyes and stands before the gate with his hands behind his back, as if facing a firing squad. His turban is shaped to a point like a ship's prow. But when she says that her uncle had once lived there, he searches her eyes and breaks into a smile. 'Yes, I *see*,' he says, and she wonders if he does. But he surprises her.

'Markose. Lawyer, he was. I remember,' the old man says. 'Played classical music very loud. Smoked a pipe. Spoke French when he was in the mood. Never late with rent. Always preceded by clouds of Old Spice.'

He takes her up himself and lets her in with an enormous bunch of keys. There is a large living room, two bedrooms, a couple of balconies full of potted plants. She lingers in the study and imagines her uncle as a young man, before he becomes a family legend, sitting at a desk in a house in Delhi, translating French poetry into Malayalam.

Downstairs, over tea and biscuits served by his wife, the old man tells her how his family had been forced out of their home in Lahore after Partition, how they arrived in Safdarjung Enclave, originally a colony of refugees from the part of India they now called Pakistan. 'And now the Pakistanis are everywhere,' he says, 'disguising themselves as vegetable sellers and chauffeurs. Even as chief ministers and journalists.' Here his voice falters. But when he talks of events from half a century ago, his memory is perfect.

'Some of us grew Hitler moustaches. Did you know that?'

Chachiamma shakes her head.

'As a protest against the British. My enemy's enemy is my friend and all that rot.'

'Not rot, Harinder,' says his wife. 'There's some truth in those sayings, that's why they are sayings.'

'Of course, of course. Churchill was a slug. Fat drunk fellow. Starved three million people to death. Blamed the dead. Said we breed like rabbits. Said the famine had nothing to do with his decision not to send food. Any wonder the Hitler moustache was popular among Indians?'

'Tell her about your brother.'

'Died in the war, fighting for the British. My brother's death affected me more than Partition. Worse for me.'

'He still dreams about it, don't you?'

'When I shut my eyes, the same picture is there. My brother in a tank. Fire around him but no panic in his eyes, not yet.'

He gets up all of a sudden. She notices how tall he is. Then, as if forgetting why he stood, he lowers himself once more to the sofa.

'We had to leave our old home in Lahore. It will always be home for me. Not like this Delhi,' he says.

'He went back,' says his wife.

'Two years after Partition, I went back. There was a boy there, said his mother was British and his father Muslim. He asked if I wanted a cup of tea. When I was served in the silver tea set with my family monogram, I knew I was homeless. I wanted to tell the boy's mother who was only a little older than me that I'd fought for the British in Italy. I wanted to tell her my brother had died and I'd been in a hospital for three years and had only now come home to find my home was gone. But when the lady asked if I had been a soldier once, all I could say was yes and drink my tea quickly. Too quickly. I burnt my tongue.'

In November the air turns so toxic people begin to leave the city, citing the pollution index which is around 400 and not likely to come down. Friends move to Bombay, Goa and Bangalore. Others leave the country altogether. As she watches the air filtering through the cotton gauze curtains they'd bought together when they first moved in, she understands that breathing is now an existential choice, equivalent to smoking a pack of cigarettes a day, without the pleasures thereof. To breathe or not to breathe? Then, one January morning, just after air purifiers have been delivered for each room, Priya makes her announcement.

'I have to tell you something,' she says.

'Oh, dear god, what is it?' says Chachiamma, fearing the worst, carcinogens come to roost from the toxic air, a lump in the breast, bad news from unforeseen prognosticators, a sudden falling out of lust, never mind love … and as it turns out, the last diagnosis is the most accurate.

'I applied to SOAS,' says Priya with an apologetic grin, 'for a year-long master's in international relations.'

'Now there's a twist I didn't see coming.'

'I was sure I wouldn't get in, which is why I didn't mention it.'

'Well, thanks for the consideration.'

'So the thing is…'

'You've been accepted.'

'I have, I've been accepted! I still can't believe it, really. I'll go home first, spend some time with the folks. They want me to fly to London early, stay with friends and, you know, get acclimatized.'

'Which friends?'

'Julia and Abeba.'

A couple, world music proponents, who visited Delhi the year before and stayed with them for two long weeks, until Chachiamma was sick of the sound of the djembe and the didgeridoo and the kalimba and, most of all, the sitar.

'Ah, of course, your dear friends from the international lesbian circuit.'

'The way you say *lesbian*, like you're not one. You're more lesbian than anyone I know, Chachi, you just present like you're not.'

Chachiamma is speechless with something like grief.

'Why didn't you tell me?' is all she can say.

Priya offers several answers but not one that makes any sense. After her lover's departure – tearless, coldly efficient, a relief for them both – Chachiamma misses Priya's mouthful of teeth, her gangly and undernourished legs, the way she lies in bed, supine and passive, expecting everything to be done to her, the obvious ADHD and the flashes of intelligence. She misses the very qualities of Priya that she found annoying when they were together.

But in less than a month, she gives up the apartment and moves to Mamalassery to live with her parents. She finds herself back on the dating circuit, with one not hugely significant difference. 'I've been shocked straight,' she tells anyone who asks, 'I might give guys another go.' When her parents set up a match with a fellow from the right background, she surprises herself by agreeing to meet him and by agreeing, almost enthusiastically, to marry him. They are in the living room of his family home in Cochin. When she bows her head in assent to his parents' proposal, she isn't addressing them, or her husband, or her own parents, who are in the room with her. She is addressing someone five thousand miles away, Priya, and imagining her former lover's face when she hears the news.

He goes online and buys round-trip tickets, Algeciras–Tangier–Algeciras, and arranges a day trip from Tangier to Chefchaouen in the mountains. They'll return to Algeciras by the last ferry. She already knows it will be a rushed, anxious trip and she doesn't want to go. She wants to explore Tangier. Port town she's read about and never imagined she would visit. But her husband wants a *tour*. He wants to be guided, to be part of a group and see the sights. That isn't the worst of it. The incomparable worst is the way he reduces a place to sound bites from the internet that kill any mystery it might hold.

'Everything is blue,' he says. 'The whole city, even the flowerpots and streets. Can you imagine?'

'Oh yes.'

'Built in the fourteen hundreds and painted blue half a century later. Symbolizes God looking upon the earth and painting his colours on all that he sees. That's why the roofs are blue.'

'If God's colour is blue, why...'

'The streets and walls and houses, brilliantly blue. Symbolic!'

'How much do you think we'll see in one afternoon?'

'Enough. They wouldn't offer a tour otherwise. It's only a two-hour drive from Tangier up into the mountains of Rif.'

'How much will we see of Tangier if it's a two-hour trip to Rif and a two-hour trip back?'

He clicks on a picture of a hill crowded with flat-roofed buildings painted blue and white and pink.

'Oh, enough, enough, I'm sure,' he says.

His interest in travel and his admiration for her posts as an influencer – the reasons she'd accepted his parents' proposal. Even if there were red flags at the very first conversation. Their respective families had left them alone in the living room. They talked about Ladakh, how it was snowed in all year round, accessible only during the summer months. 'Imagine going in the good weather and staying until the roads cleared eight months later,' she said, 'what an experience!' His face registered not delight but horror. Chachiamma ignored the flag, the *tiny* flag, but she should have known. And now here they are, on a ferry from Europe to Africa, up on deck looking for photo opportunities.

'There might be whales too,' he says. 'Talk about maximizing one's Morocco experience!'

He has his headphones on, and she guesses he is blasting his disgusting Steel Panther playlist. She watches his mouth curve downward as he turns in a tight arc to take panorama pictures on his phone. Of what? Perhaps he really believes an obliging whale will surface for his camera. She prays nothing will show. No dolphin or flying fish. Not a single one of God's good sea creatures. 'Don't, oh God, please,' she says. Uncharitable prayer, but she has her reasons.

What she likes most about travel is the act of travel, being somewhere unreachable where no one will find her. She'll take a picture and post it and that is that. She is gone. Now, all has changed. Her husband posts several times a day. He tags their location, every bar and restaurant and bus station and airport, all of it on his feed for everyone to see. She is no longer off the grid. She is of the grid, another pin on a vast map of pins, watched, triangulated, known at all times.

She tastes salt and watches the churn left by the ferry as Spain recedes behind a veil of spray, each drop an element in a pattern of disappointment. The dress she'd worn on the flight to Madrid feels stale against her skin, as if a layer of grit has grown inside the fabric.

She goes to find a restroom.

AT THE METAL STAIRCASE, HALF A dozen people cluster around some sort of tour guide, a white-haired woman with a cane whose eyes are hidden behind impenetrable dark glasses.

She is like no guide Chachiamma has ever heard.

'... that we're all different,' she says. 'But are we really? And if so, how so? I hear a question these days, people asking: Where are you from? The reply is always one or two words, always inaccurate. Nobody is from one place. Where we are really from is where we're going now. This body of water wasn't always here. It appeared after Europe broke off from the mother continent. By this, I mean a very simple thing. This journey is a return, and it might be the single most important journey you will make.'

Here the woman pauses, and the people listening look at each other, at the sky, at the brilliant water. Some wander away to take pictures.

She says, 'Like the Suez Canal, this is a mental waterbody more than a physical one. It separates Africa from Asia and Europe and underlines the fact that we're connected.'

Again she pauses, moving her head from side to side, as if she knows exactly where the ferry is in relation to port. Then she taps her cane and continues.

'The origin story of mankind says our species descended from a hominid group that lived in Africa some two hundred and fifty thousand years ago. Some say East Africa, others South Africa. But always they point to one spot, usually Botswana, as the cradle of the race.'

Chachiamma strains to hear, alone above the noise of the ferry as the soft pulse of the voice draws her close. The others in the group look on blandly, without reproach, their faces impassive or bored. They have no inkling how extraordinary are the woman's words.

'Some years ago,' she says, 'fossils were found at Jebel Irhoud, three hundred thousand years old, the oldest of our species. So now, they say, we must add a new region to the cradle theory. North-west Africa, the exact spot we are approaching. Why should these theories be in conflict? Isn't it possible Homo sapiens lived in different parts of the continent we now know as Africa? Groups of early humans who would meet and mate, exchange blood and weapons, DNA, ideas, then pull apart for whatever reason, say climate, or hunger?'

The more she speaks, the more Chachiamma is determined to stay within earshot. What she is saying applies to everyone, but especially to her, Chachiamma.

'I *am* blind,' says the woman, 'which means I'm less prone to the sway of appearance, eye colour, skin colour, body type, fashion. All those things you put so much stock in.'

Here she pauses and lifts her face and nods.

'Now,' she says, 'may I have two volunteers?'

Chachiamma puts her hand in the air without meaning to. Realizing the woman can't see, she says, 'I volunteer.'

'Who else?' says the blind woman.

'Me,' says the man closest to her. A scruffy old man with grey-blonde hair and a sparse beard.

'Someone take my cane for a moment,' says the woman. She places a hand on each of their faces. 'I can guess that you are a woman and you are not. You have two eyes each, well-shaped skulls, prominent jaws, and smaller faces than Homo erectus. I'd say you're almost identical.'

Chachiamma looks out at the water, but soon enough her gaze returns to the woman whose hand stays on her cheek.

'And now I want to talk about dogs,' the woman says, reclaiming her cane and tapping twice on the deck. 'Look at the enormous range within the basic motif. How different they are, in size, in temperament, in shape and purpose. I compare dogs to humans, and I am struck once again at how similar we are. It should be clear that our differences are of colour more than shape or size. Colour.' She is silent for a moment, her head tilted, listening. 'But wait, we're about to dock. I will continue my lecture on the return journey if any of you are here then. In the meanwhile, I wish you a pleasant visit to Tangier.'

Chachiamma knows exactly what to tell her husband, who is still on deck hunting dolphins. Her period is upon her, she says. She'll stay on the ferry and meet him at the hotel in Algeciras. Her husband, always uncomfortable with talk of a woman's period, is surprisingly amenable to the idea of taking the day trip alone. He might even be relieved.

On the return, the woman speaks about borders. How important they are for a nation's sense of its identity. How fragile is that identity. Why it is that fraternal or neighbouring regions have the worst relationships, Israel and Palestine, for instance, or Pakistan and India, or China and Japan. It isn't territorial rivalry these countries are engaged in but an imagined battle for survival. The woman takes a seat and seems more relaxed now. Her audience has thinned to three people. Chachiamma sits beside her and feels comforted for the first time in days. She stops hearing the meaning of the words. She hears only cadence and pitch.

At lunch, the woman goes to the bar and Chachiamma follows. Expertly using her cane to gauge direction, moving more confidently than the people around her, she takes a seat near a window that looks out on a sea turned slate and choppy. The waiter brings a glass of wine. 'May I join you,' Chachiamma says, 'I was at your lecture.' The woman doesn't reply but takes a sip of wine and sighs. Reluctantly, she speaks, 'You may sit.'

Chachiamma blurts out her question.

'Do you need an assistant or a researcher, photographer, anything at all? I'd be happy to help.'

Silently she says, please, please say yes.

'No,' says the woman. 'I'm in no need of assistance.'

'Oh, I don't mean you need assistance. I can see you don't. It's just that I found your talk useful and...'

'Useful? Of all things, why useful?'

'I don't know.'

'I'm of no use, not to you, not to anyone.'

'I just want to help.'

'If you really want to help, leave me alone.'

The blind woman's head swings from side to side as if she were being slapped. But she doesn't get up and she doesn't ask Chachiamma to leave. The ferryboat rocks a little, buffeted by small waves the wind picks up. The woman's expression is so alert it makes Chachiamma's skin prickle.

She goes to the restroom where she splashes water on her face and examines her eyes. She sees the green tracery of veins under the skin of the eyelids, the hard-working brows, the lashes that protect the eyes' delicate tissues from dust. She sees that her arms are extensions of her eyes. And her fingers, how fragile they are, and necessary. Inside her, she sees the cisterns and viaducts of a city. The nature of the lie she told her husband strikes her anew, for she sees her baby's new heartbeat coming into rhythm. For two days, she has known. To be with child at such a time, by such a man, what a feat of bad judgement. Impossible to undo. She shakes out a cigarette and remembers she is pregnant and tosses the pack into the trash, followed by her new Bic. She'll stop smoking.

When the ferry docks at Algeciras, she is in the thick of the crowd waiting to disembark. The faces around her are distracted or excited or worried. It isn't her usual practice to stare at strangers. Now, because of the blind woman's intimate knowledge of faces, now she cannot look away. The eyes of each man and woman strike her like blows. 'Eyes reveal,' she whispers. Her own eyes expose her, allow passers-by to see her deepest thoughts. They open her to danger. She digs in her purse for the sunglasses she'd found at the airport, cheap plastic shades with palm trees at the temples, puts them on and feels infinitely better, invincible, like the blind woman. The press of people waiting to exit grows worse. From all sides they come with their backpacks and cameras, clutching giant mineral water bottles and sheaves of travel documents. Desperate to be saved. How fearful they are. And at the last moment, as the crowd reaches the gate, she turns and struggles back to the upper deck. There she waits until the engines start, and the tears come to her eyes.

She imagines staying on the ferry as it plies ceaselessly between Europe and Africa. Her baby will be a citizen of no country except the stretch of deep water between continents, an in-betweener like her. For now, both she and the baby are hungry. At the bar, she buys a plate of couscous and the waiter gives her a complimentary cookie. She takes the table by the window and treats herself to a glass of wine. Later, she stretches out on a bench on the upper deck and lets the rocking of the boat lull her. Sleep comes, deep and dreamless. In the morning, when the blind woman arrives, Chachiamma will be ready. She'll ask if she might join her at lunch. The blind woman may agree and Chachiamma may become a fixture at her lectures. Why not? There is nothing to stop her, except money. In her purse is a small wad of dollars, euros, rupees, a credit card. The cash will run out soon enough. By then, she'll know what to do.

Two months later, they are at Mui Ne beach in Vietnam. She wants to swim, but the water near the hotel is filthy with garbage. There is a black flag and a sign that says swimming is dangerous. They walk to the other end, because a swim cheers her up like nothing else. She thinks it will be good for her in her new state. Of which her husband is still unaware. So oblivious is he. So ignorant of morning sickness and the thousand changes. She doesn't want to tell him. It's a private state of communion between her and the baby taking shape inside her. Why should she tell? Her husband doesn't deserve it. All he deserves to know is that the marriage is over.

The midday heat has lost its mildness and begun to burn. The air turns from honey to treacle and the great fist of the sun wraps around her head. She should have brought a hat. Shielding her eyes with her hand, she becomes aware of a couple a little ahead of them. Tattooed and oiled, young, in sunglasses and too-tight swimsuits. Something about them makes her not want to get too close. Something about the scowl the man aims at her husband. They are the only other people on the beach. She knows why they are annoyed. The sand is white and the blue sea stretches to the horizon. There are sails on the water and not a cloud in the sky. It could have been Croatia or Estonia or the Mediterranean, but it isn't. It decidedly is not. Because she and her husband, two brown people, have marred the perfect afternoon. When they come to a rock pool, the couple stop. The man writes something on the sand with a stick he's carrying in the belt loop of his denim cut-offs. They are there a long time, working on the sand.

Chachiamma waits until they go further down the beach. Then she walks along the surf-line until she comes to the spot where the couple had been sand-writing. On the clean beach, deep trenches have been dug in the shape of a swastika. Two Cyrillic names lie inside a circle embossed with curlicues and flowers. She feels the trenched swastika deep in her abdomen and places a hand on her belly to steady herself. What does the baby, the soon-to-be baby register? The world is full of people and people are full of hate. Surely it is no reason for surprise.

She tells her husband, 'There's something you should know.'

THE GARDENER

Bangalore, 2020

'At Goethe's request the Padua gardener cut from the fan palm an entire sequence of modifications which Goethe carried away with him in several pasteboard containers, where they lasted several years. As for the palm tree, it still stands in the Padua botanical gardens despite numerous intervening wars and revolutions.'

PETER TOMPKINS & CHRISTOPHER BIRD,

The Secret Life of Plants

THEY ARE IN BANGALORE WHEN the country shuts down.

She's planted butter and jackfruit trees that fruit once a year and need no upkeep. The butter fruit is still growing, has already surpassed fifty feet, gives more than two hundred fruit in August and September. Butter fruit: the local name. She likes it better than avocado which combines aqua and cato to wrongly evoke a wallop, a heavy slug of water. The butter fruit isn't watery by any stretch. The massive jackfruit reminds her of Mamalassery, where the tree grows in abundance. She likes to say that the Portuguese who sailed into Calicut in the fifteenth century gave the jack tree its English name by mispronouncing the Malayalam, chakka. And there are silk-cotton trees that tower above all others, just coming into fruit and bright red flower, each a self-contained system with its own bird and insect life. Behind the house, a rain tree as hardy as the avocado and jackfruit, its multiple roots seeking moisture at an ever-growing radius wider by far than its canopy. But the flower beds need attention, as do the orchids in coconut shells she's suspended from a home-made trellis.

For most of March and April, when the silk-cotton trees are in bloom, the gardener Govindappa comes to tend the flowers and dwarf palms and birds of paradise. Marooned by the lockdown, he is stuck in the city. They fall into a routine. Ammu and George help with the clearing of dead leaves from the terracotta tiles on the patio. Later, she brings him coffee and the little gardener will squat on the terrace with the steel glass in his small, hard hands. He speaks haltingly, disconnectedly. If his clothes are unkempt and mud-stained, the moustache is well tended, the white hair recently cut and styled. He looks to be around sixty. His conversation doesn't vary but circles around anxiety. The gardening work has dried up. Soon he'll have to give up the rented place, go home. But how? Public transport is cancelled. Private cars aren't allowed on the roads. He'll have to join the river of migrants walking to their home towns.

Originally from a village near the Burmese border, Govindappa's ancestors left home in search of better like everyone else, moved south because they heard good things about Kempegowda, the wily old chieftain who started things off in the sixteenth century with a wholly unremarkable mud fort. He then sent open invitations to the nation's traders to bring their families and settle, which they did, whole neighbourhoods coming to be known by the goods they produced, Akkipet and Ragipet and Chickpet, named for rice and ragi and markets of all kinds. The Kalsis, expert tent-pitchers, invaluable in battle, settled in a neighbourhood that came to be known as Kalsipalya.

Govindappa tried to find out why his ancestors left their village. Why Karnataka instead of another state? How did they come by their names? Who decided they'd be artisans? No records had been kept. All he could find were family stories and legends. He knew it was thanks to Kempegowda that his grandmother still had her fingers. The chieftain made it illegal to chop two fingers from a widow's hand, which had been the practice all along. If you lost your husband, you lost your fingers, or your life. Until her last illness, his grandmother invoked Kempegowda's name as if she were saying the name of God. As a boy, he thought the name was a prayer. She said their ancestors found the south of Karnataka too warm in the summer and too dusty all year round. They missed the mountains, so they went as far north as possible. Two years later, they settled in Bidar, a hill city at the state's northernmost point, and they became artisans of Bidriware, the only Hindu family in what was a Muslim craft, working silver into earrings and hookahs, puzzle boxes and ornamental bowls, vases filigreed with stylized Persian roses, poppies, creeper vines. Their livelihoods fluctuated as the demand for Bidriware rose and fell. This was when Govindappa's father had his idea. His son would study landscape architecture, not Bidriware. Where his ancestors used a chisel and hammer to engrave silvery roses and ivory vines, Govindappa would create living trees and flowers, conjure them out of the soil, out of the air, with nothing but his two hands. He'd never be out of work.

And that was how he became the first of his family to come to Bangalore. He was young, awed by the connecting networks of roads planned around the great gardens that took up six hundred acres in the heart of town, Lalbaug and Cubbon Park. He learned about his new home. The continuous wave of people who moved here with their languages and customs, the second largest migrant population in the country. About half the city was made up of outsiders. He wasn't the only one from a distant place. But in the space of thirty years, everything turned on its head. Building constructed on building. Green spaces gone. Concrete everywhere. There wasn't much work for a landscaper now that the landscapes had been paved over. He felt as though he was coming out of a deep sleep at the age of fifty-five, to a new world in which nothing made sense, reaching for the comfort of root and branch but finding only thin and thinner air. He became a gardener.

After the lockdown, Govindappa continues to work on the house and one or two others. But in the last days of April, he disappears. Ammu makes enquiries and learns that he's set off for Bidar on foot, a journey of seven hundred kilometres. Desperate and without money, migrant families are on the killing road, inadequately masked, carrying utensils and babies, plastic bags, bedding, wheeled suitcases. Perishing along the way.

Ammu and George wonder if they'll see him again.

For those months, it seems the city's sole inhabitants are dogs and police. When the curfew is lifted for a few hours each morning, they walk around the neighbourhood. George takes nothing for granted. The sky clear of pollution. Roads clear of cars. Mind clear of thought. There are few pedestrians on those mornings, only the poor buying provisions for the week, wondering when the money will run out. Even the street dogs slink away abashed, knowing something is off. It may be the first time he's looked closely at the city's architecture. The weird mix of Victoriana via the British and the Islamic flourishes left by the Mughals. He thinks of it as the local style, Baburi Gothic or Dravidian Grotesque. Some of the older buildings have become ruins, deserted by their civil service habitués. The roofs have caved in, leaving the elegant interiors open to the marauding elements. Weeds devour the windows and skylights.

On the way home, they see a coffin propped against a wall on their lane. Then another. Cheap plywood coffins light as air. It becomes a familiar sight as time passes and more people die, as cemeteries fill beyond capacity and the coffin-makers die, as people dispense with coffins altogether. Burial, too. The dead are cremated wherever there is space. Or they are thrown into rivers and drainage canals and left on the sidewalks outside hospitals and crematoria. As always, they are quickly forgotten. But in the early days of the new era, the sight of a cardboard coffin against someone's front gate makes the passer-by stop and fix it with his survivor's gaze.

One evening in late March, she opens the screen door to the kitchen. On a patch of grass there are flame trees in red bloom. Kids play basketball, their screams so joyful they seem to come from another world. She is among streets emptied of people, in a city in lockdown, she's forgotten there is basketball and joy. Later that night, she goes to the short metal fence that sets off the trees and basketball hoop. The kids and their excitement, the sound of a ball hitting a backboard, the heat of the day, all of it seems hopelessly distant. Then, very close, she sees a ginger cat in the moonlight and knows her as the stray that has been visiting the house for a year now, long enough that she's been given a name. Virginia Floof. There is no food for her, so she sets out a bowl of milk which Virginia sniffs but doesn't touch. Ammu is rewarded with a look of surprise, a question in the slate eyes. What makes you think I like milk?

That week, the government orders the reopening of essential businesses. Citizens are allowed to shop but can't leave their neighbourhoods on pain of police harassment. Groceries, cashpoints, chemist and household supplies are to be found within two kilometres of their homes. At a small department store off the main road, she finds fresh fruit, packaged bread, country eggs, tomatoes – and a bag of cat food. Virginia grows to depend on the brand. From the moment Ammu brings home the crunchy salmon-flavoured treats, things change. A connection is established.

What does it teach you to know a cat? The lesson she learns concerns her place in the hierarchy. She is a small and dispensable part of the great cycle. With Virginia, her role is not that of benefactor. She is there to serve, Virginia to be served. If sometimes Ammu looks to her for appreciation, for acknowledgement or understanding, she knows soon enough that it won't come. At those times, she remembers a song her son used to play, by a raggedy-voiced singer who complained about a lack of affection, gratitude and love. Your loyalty is not to me, he cried, but to the stars above. This doesn't seem to her a cause for complaint. Who are we to demand love, even from our own children? Everything is finite. From Virginia, she understands that the world remains unchanged, if only in the small ways that carry us forward. The living live, contingent: humans in their confusion, animals in their certainty. A cat's attention is narrowed to the moment and its thousand possibilities. Virginia doesn't know there is a plague in the world, that livelihoods have been lost, that the leaders of the nation are beyond reason and compassion. She doesn't care. Ammu notes the way her ears are tuned to the sounds around her. Crows and crickets. An occasional car. The deep thud of a generator. Scree of hawk from far above the trees. Someone's quiet voice. The way she filters these sounds, alert to predators, the way she tenses and eats, these are the ways in which she is connected to the world, and that connection is enough. How she longs to be Virginia. But since she can't be her, she is happy to feed her.

There's no greater act of optimism than to feed a cat.

Some imagine they are powerless. They imagine a villain into existence. A minority community with its own dietary and marriage laws. Having found an imaginary villain, imaginary justice is enacted. A man is lynched. The lynching becomes a spectacle. The body is displayed on a rural road where the killers pose with their trophy. The image is shared a hundred times, a thousand times, a hundred thousand times. The leaders of the nation are pleased. The killers are rewarded. The cycle continues.

Early the following April, the lockdown is lifted and Govindappa returns. The lawn has overgrown in some places and dried out in others. The creeper on the patio arbour is festooned with dead leaves and the butter tree is much the worse for wear. The year of lockdown has afflicted plant life as well. The gardener falls into his old routine. Work, a coffee break, more work, and then around lunchtime he'll go to his next job.

The story of his journey to Bidar emerges as the days pass. It had been more dangerous than they'd imagined. At first, he'd been able to cover only around twenty-five kilometres a day. There were other migrants walking home, and some of them had longer journeys than he. Entire families took turns to ride a single bicycle. For long stretches, he saw no sign of habitation except the painted numbers on the trees. To distract himself, he counted each tree to make sure no mistake had been made in the numbering. At night, he slept on the side of the road. In the morning, a biscuit or a handful of peanuts and some water. From time to time, he was stopped and questioned at makeshift checkposts. Sometimes, he saw a truck or an ambulance. He didn't make good time. He had a backpack with clothes and foodstuffs, his watch, family photos, a Ganesh figurine. His choice of footwear was a mistake. He'd taken only his good Batas, the formal leather lace-ups he wore to job interviews. He couldn't leave them behind. On the second day, he developed blisters. Govindappa tried to pray but the blisters made it difficult to walk while reciting the old slokas. Instead, he concentrated on his breathing, on putting one foot in front of the other.

It was the kindness of villagers that saved him. He exchanged his stiff formal shoes for tennis shoes one size too big and stuffed the toe with newspaper. This increased the distance he covered to thirty-five or forty kilometres a day. He'd start at six in the morning when it was still cool and stop for a rest around eleven. Then start again around four and keep going until the sun went down. Five or six hours of walking at a moderate pace, surviving on biscuits and water and the dried fruits he carried from Bangalore, conserving his strength. There were other dangers. Some were robbed. Of what? What more could be taken from them? Govindappa slept with a hand on his money and his backpack under his head. But his hardships were nothing compared to some of the others.

After a week of walking, he'd reached only as far as Anantapur. It was dry and very hot. The gardener was tired in his bones. He squinted at the bright summer sun and examined the trees by the side of the road, which were like Govindappa himself, knotted and old and alive yet liable to keel over at any moment. When the sun went down, exhausted he sat by the side of the road, not far from a group of men and boys who had also given in to exhaustion. A container truck stopped. The driver demanded five thousand rupees per person. Around twenty of them got in. Inside, it was dark and close with a single, grilled opening for ventilation. The driver stopped only twice in three days, at night, to allow the men to relieve themselves. The world became tiny, reduced to the sound of faulty brakes, the sensation of the truck coming to a stop, silence as they waited for the driver to open the back. When he stepped into the road and looked up at the stars, the air smelled of grass, laburnums and death. He thought, 'It doesn't matter whether you're in South India or the Himalayas, the same stars sail above.' He forgot his plight and became one with the earth and sky. He forgot the world of men, or he forgot what kind of men make up the world. But they never let you forget for long. Because it was time to get back into the truck and continue north. At five the next morning, the police stopped them at a checkpost. The driver said he was carrying vegetables. They waited, trying not to make a sound, trying not to breathe. Some money must have changed hands. It seemed like hours, but it must have been only minutes before the truck was moving again.

'We were all of us in the same trouble,' says Govindappa, 'together on the endless road, sent home by cruel men who didn't care about the poor. Maybe I was expecting brotherly compassion. But hardship made our differences plain. All of us had to worry about food, water, falling down from tiredness. Some of us also had to worry about being attacked by our fellows. I'm thinking about the two boys. I wish I could forget, but I see them in my dreams. It started with the usual jokes. They pointed at Shafiq and his brother Imtiaz, called them beef-eaters, knocked off their skullcaps. Skullcaps. Imagine that. All it took to make them our enemies was headgear. Boys of sixteen and fifteen. Somebody slapped one of them and it was as if a signal had been sent and received. Hard blows to the head and throat. One fell and they kicked him from all sides. I never saw the knife. Then it was there. Stuck to the hilt again and again. The blood took a second to spout and then it fell on all of us in that small space. Blood spray on my face, my hair. I couldn't understand the smell. Like rusted metal and sewage. By the time the driver heard the commotion and stopped, Shafiq was dead. Twenty-six holes in him. Some of the wounds just small slits in the groin and neck. But those cuts bled the most. The murderer knew how to use a knife, he'd done it before. I don't know how to describe the look on his face. Excitement, yes, and joy, but also pride. He'd done his work and done it well. He brandished his knife and ran. Imtiaz had been stabbed too, but his cries were for his older brother, heart-rending cries I won't forget.

'The police came. We stood there in our ignorance, and they questioned us, gently. Gentle questions and ignorant answers. I expected interrogations, blows, more blows. The murderer was out there somewhere, the diligent stabber, the hard-working, joyful killer, out there and free to roam. Nobody looked for him. Nobody wanted to question him. Even now he must be roaming. The next day they let us go. I wasn't far from home. What happened then? Nothing. Nothing happened. Oh, I've reached my home at last, I thought. It was no comfort.'

Ammu understands. The lust for blood is an old lust. But his mention of home tugs at her and will not let her go. When will she see it again, the house on River-of-Three-Rivers?

RETURN AND END

Dessie, 1962 | Mamalassery, 2021

'Do that today which you would keep for tomorrow. Do that in the forenoon what you would keep for the afternoon. Death does not wait for anyone to see whether she has or has not performed her task.'

Mahabharata, xii, 322.73

AT THE MARKET, SHE SPOTS A woman wearing a crazy blue smock. On the chest and skirt and sleeves, four-pointed yellow crosses that remind her of the orthodox crosses of Kerala. They call it a habesha kemis. Habshi dress. Similar in cut to the salwar kameez she used to wear in college.

From where, she asks the woman, using her hands.

'You'll find the better shops at the opposite end of the market,' the woman replies in perfectly good English.

Uma buys three, the least shiny of those on offer, then wanders around the unruly colours on display. The stalls are little more than sacks spread on a stack of wood with a handful of papayas and lemons and vegetables she can't name. Or tarps on the ground with piles of red onions, potatoes, carrots. She sees a bundle of sugar-cane stalks and the sudden taste of cane juice is in her mouth. The vendor cuts one and strips the skin. She chews standing up with her eyes closed as she had as a child. Hands sticky with juice, she drifts around the market with no purpose, mindful that it is the first time she's taken pleasure in her surroundings since arriving in Ethiopia with her husband eight months earlier. Husband. Her husband is waiting. Reluctantly, she walks to the depot. A blue bus with curtained windows waits for passengers to the university. She sits in front and dozes and wakes thinking she's missed her stop, but the bus hasn't moved.

When she gets home, he is reading a James Hadley Chase thriller on the couch in the front room. On the coffee table is the day's bottle of Johnnie Walker. Almost empty. There is spittle on his chin and his thick fingers turn the pages as she takes out her shopping. He offers no opinion about the habesha kemis or her adventure at the market. By dinner, he is unsteady on his feet and before she's finished the dishes, he is asleep. She tries on a kemis with a pattern of gold crosses against a navy blue field. How comfortable it is, like wearing air. With the protection of the cross, she can go back to the market near the bus depot. What would it mean to have a spot there and sell something, fruits or vegetables, and think only about the day's produce?

Bliss. It would be bliss.

Upstairs, she finds him sprawled across the bed with one muscular arm flung across his eyes. If she lies beside him, he'll reach for her without a word. As if he were mute or hypnotized. But tonight, protected by the habesha kemis, she goes carefully down the steep staircase and sleeps on the couch and dreams of camels abandoned on the streets of a city, hemmed in by traffic and buildings and their own bewilderment. When she climbs on the back of one of the animals, it leaps enormous distances if she only says a word. It is the most useful word in the world, but she can't remember it when she wakes.

He is upstairs at the sink, the day's first bottle open on the toothbrush shelf. It's how he likes to start the day, sipping while he shaves. When he leaves for his job at the university, she puts a shawl over the kemis and steps out of the house and walks until she finds a place that sells coffee. She sits in a yard in the sun and watches a small girl wash a handful of beans over a patch of mint, careful not to waste a drop of water. The girl smiles, conscious that Uma is watching. She spreads freshly cut grass on the ground and burns small pieces of stone the colour of faded roses. As the dizzying, unmistakable smell of frankincense rises into the air, Uma shuts her eyes. The smell of Kerala's churches has followed her to Dessie, like the crosses and the sugar cane. Her childhood has followed her.

At last come the tears she has kept at bay for a week, for a month, and she weeps without care. The girl continues her work, roasting the beans in a long-handled pan and grinding them in a pestle. She beckons to Uma, gesturing with a handful of ground coffee. Uma inhales the aroma her mother used to describe as 'angel's sweat'. The girl puts the powder into a pot and lets it boil, once, once more, and a third time, and then she pours the coffee from high in the air into a small cup and adds a teaspoon of sugar and hands it to Uma. The brew is oily and thick. She drinks slowly, disbelievingly. When she finishes, the girl pours more.

By the third cup, Uma's tears have stopped.

In her second trimester, when the worst of the nausea has passed, she starts down the stairs one night and hears Jacob calling from the bedroom. 'No,' she says, 'I sleep better on the couch.' He takes her by the hand and she pulls away, and the momentum of it carries her tumbling down. She feels the baby hit the edge of the bottom step. Esha is born with her legs twisted at the knees, unable to walk without assistance but otherwise perfectly healthy and happy. The routine of Esha's care becomes part of their lives. Making sure one of them is always with her, shaping their day around her needs.

Around this time, Uma begins to visit the church. A bare round building in a nondescript neighbourhood of old houses and stray dogs and trash on the curbs. She goes to the church on Saturdays when Jacob doesn't have to be at the university and can stay with Esha. She always takes the front pew because she likes the picture of Jesus and Mary placed to the side of the pulpit, their faces as dark as hers, as dark as any of the people around her. Mary holds her baby to her chest and carries a staff and a bundle. An old man follows close, also carrying bundles and a staff. Uma has looked at the picture a hundred times. She knows there is a message for her, but she doesn't know what it might be. It is like no portrait of Jesus and Mary and Joseph she's ever seen. Skin the colour of coffee with a drop of milk, hair black and wiry, eyes haunted by grief. Their robes are worn. Anyone can see they are tired and footsore from long travel.

One morning, she watches a family at the church. Mother, father, young daughter, newly arrived from somewhere to the north, their belongings on the floor. They are praying together, the aura of Elsewhere upon them. Now she understands the message the picture holds. Mary and Joseph were migrants when Jesus was born, and for years afterwards. Jesus was a migrant. His family went from one place to another to stay alive.

Movement. Movement is God's message. This is what they tried to hide, the well-fed priests of the grand churches of her childhood. They didn't want it known that God is also God to the poor and the displaced, more so to them than to the rich who are comfortable and protected and stay in one place for reasons of property or marriage or laziness. Here, the priest didn't stand at a raised pulpit above the congregation. He stands without finery among the people. The church too boasts no finery, no decoration other than the picture and a simple white cross. It is the way: closer to God.

'I want to go home,' she tells Jacob that evening.

'What's wrong with Dessie? It's home now.'

'Not for me. I'm pregnant again.'

He rises, happily drunk, and says, 'Clean-shave.'

'If it's a girl, we call her Chachiamma after your mother.'

'If it's a boy?'

'Joseph.'

Ammu and George set off for Mamalassery. Ammu wants to see the river and the house. She says:

'Possibly ... I mean, probably for the last time.'

They plan to stay two weeks, but the lockdown stretches the weeks to months. When travel restrictions are lifted temporarily, I join them and we are together again at the old Anniethottam tharavad. Ammu is excited to visit, her first time in many years, though things have changed. The front courtyard is covered in moss. At the centre is a stone basin of stagnant water, an experiment in goldfish rearing. But the fish have died and unknown ferns grow wild. Uma has let the water become a home to river mosquitoes the size of bluebottles. To enter, you have to cross the slippery courtyard and skirt the basin of mosquitoes. In the morning, there are red spots on the bed sheet where they sipped at you through the night. And there are bees on the porch around a clay pot that serves as a hive. Uma squeezes the honey with ungloved hands. Bees buzz around her.

'God is the author of my life,' she says. 'He won't let them bite me.'

'Really, Uma,' says George. 'Must you talk like that?'

But she is right. The bees and mosquitoes leave her alone.

'We all know the real reason for the bees,' George says later.

'Please keep your voice down,' says Ammu. 'I don't want her to hear your wild theories.'

'She's trained the bees and the mosquitoes to bite guests only. She doesn't want anyone coming to visit.'

'You must be writing an article in your head. Only reason for this kind of talk.'

'What?' says George, his selective hearing kicking in.

But most of the time calm prevails.

Ammu, George and Uma say they want to visit the St Francis church at Fort Kochi where Markose is buried. Jacob has other things to do, he says. And so it falls to me to drive the tank-like black Ambassador, rarely used, dripping rust, forgotten under a plastic sheet in the garage. But the old car starts on the first try.

'Warhorse,' says Jacob proudly. 'Simply unstoppable.'

The cemetery is full of well-tended gravestones and crypts with the names and dates of long-gone Englishmen felled by archaic ailments, by dropsy and ague and gout. A plaque announces that Vasco da Gama was buried at the church. It seems correct somehow that he'd died at the very place about which he'd made one mistaken assumption after the other. That the city of Calicut is inhabited by Christians. That they clip their hair short or shave the head, allowing a tuft to remain on the crown as a sign they're Christians. (It's a sign they're Hindu.) That the women, as a rule, are ugly, of small stature, well disposed and of mild temper, even if at first sight they seem covetous and ignorant.

It takes some time to find Markose's stone. Hidden in a corner under a sacred fig is a short white slab with dates and a single word. CRENOM!

'But what does it mean?' asks Ammu.

'It must be French,' says Uma. 'Nothing rude, I hope.'

I say: 'A contraction of Sacré Nom: as in, the sacred name of Christ. At the end of his life, when Baudelaire lost his mind, it was the only word he had left. Markose wrote about it in his book.'

'But why put a thing like that on his gravestone?'

'Isn't it obvious?' says Ammu. 'He had nothing to say and no one to say it to. That's what caused the heart attack.'

She is wearing a bracelet I haven't seen before, thin gold with a heart-shaped clasp that she lifts to her face.

'He gave it to me,' she says, 'when I got married. I almost lost it on the train to Bombay. A little girl tried to take it from me. I took it back.'

I notice the engraving – August 25, 1957 – my parents' wedding date. Wetting a handkerchief, she wipes some of the grime off the headstone. We stand around for some time and then go into the church.

The vicar's office is a whitewashed room with a large desk that holds a silver tea service and a rotary telephone. Unusually for a Kerala clergyman, he isn't fat. In fact, he is slender and alert to the eccentricity of the company that has invaded his day. We are invited to sit on overstuffed armchairs.

George says he has some questions.

'Here we go,' says Ammu. 'Prepare yourself, vicar sir.'

'Of course,' says the vicar. 'But first, welcome to the oldest European church in India.'

On the wall is a silver crucifix from which Christ regards us as we sip tea and nibble on cashew biscuits.

'Interesting that he isn't looking up to the heavens but directly at us,' says George, 'with the knowing gaze of a man abandoned on a hilltop by his only friends.'

'He must be writing some article in his head again,' says Ammu to the vicar. 'Nothing to worry.'

'But why is it called the St Francis church when he was never here? It's a bit strange,' says George.

'Strange?' says the vicar.

'Well, there's no proof St Thomas came here at all.'

'There are several Thomases in the complicated history of Indian Christianity. It's natural for us to express a reasonable doubt since we are talking about Doubting Thomas,' says the vicar, pleased with his joke. 'What if there was a mix-up, not a falsification but a mistake? What if it wasn't our St Thomas but Thomas of Canaan? We know he came to South India in the third century. Even now, the Canaanite Christians believe they are higher on the ladder and won't mingle with other Christians, especially not by marriage.'

The vicar dips a cashew biscuit into his tea and the rest of us follow suit. Tea is slurped and biscuits chewed amid grunts of pleasure.

'Marriage is a popular topic of my sermons,' says Uma suddenly. 'Do you know *Psychic Matchmaker*? Deborah lives at the famous Delray Beach. Just by holding your hands and looking into your eyes she'll find your soulmate!'

The vicar stares at Uma, then at the silver wall crucifix.

'I've also studied *I Love a Mama's Boy* in which a woman competes with a young man's mother for his affections. And of course, *90 Day Fiancé*. The hero is the K-1 visa available to foreign fiancés of US citizens. In ninety days, not a day longer, they must marry or die.'

'Out of my jurisdiction,' says the vicar to the crucifix. 'I am a vicar to two hundred families. I like to keep things simple.'

'Why is it called the St Francis church?' says George.

'When the Rajah of Cochin gave the Portuguese permission to build, in 1503, they wanted the first construction to be a church. It was dedicated to St Antony. The British rebuilt it three hundred and fifty years later and made St Francis the patron saint.'

'I want to invite you to my church,' says Uma. 'It isn't as grand as yours, but it is closer to God in simplicity.'

'What makes you think God is partial to simplicity? Unless you mean to say symmetry or sympathy, which qualities He may set store by. Simplicity on the other hand is a kind of snobbery. Which church?'

'I'm of the Pentecostal denomination,' says Uma piously.

'That's not a denomination,' says the vicar. 'That's damnation! I have questions about history, oh yes, but that doesn't mean I want to burn everything to the ground.'

'Damnation not denomination,' says George. 'Quotable quote!'

'We should join forces,' says Uma.

'I should get back to work,' says the vicar, rising to his feet.

'Nobody will blame you, vicar sir,' says Ammu.

In the car, Uma seems gleeful, singing hymns all the way. When we get to the house, she goes to her room and puts on the television and resumes her favourite pastime: interrogating the world.

George spends the evening at the dining table working on a manuscript or staring out the window, silent as usual, and I am reminded that silence is a family weapon passed down through the generations. George is a master of the discipline. Often, when I was a child, he wouldn't speak to me for days as punishment for something I'd done or not done. He wouldn't look in my direction. My confusion would give way to silence of my own. I wouldn't speak to him or look in his direction. The standoff would continue until Ammu stepped in to make peace. Over the years, silence became normal, even comforting. A long drive, the two of us, not a word spoken.

He writes by hand on sheets of recycled newsprint, cuts a section with scissors and pastes it to another sheet: his primitive editing technique. He no longer uses computers or typewriters. He is partially deaf but refuses to use a hearing aid. He giggles when embarrassed. Sometimes, I find him in the yard staring at the trees. He no longer remembers if he's taken his cancer medication the night before or if he's had breakfast. These small acts of forgetting free him. Because of his failing memory and lack of hearing, he becomes genial, very different from the humourless authoritarian I've known for most of my youth. He's forgotten how to be a bully.

Ammu and I are in the room as he works that afternoon. He writes in Malayalam, fluidly, his hand running steadily across the page. In conversation, he is frequently lost and unable to respond to a simple question. But the writing is going well. A memoir disguised as profiles of personalities he had known in his days as a young journalist in Bombay and Hong Kong.

The scratch of pen against paper ceases. He looks up from his work and scrutinizes Ammu, then me.

'Father does not speak. Mother speaks. That's why it's called mother tongue.' He giggles as if he's said something profound.

Drifts of paper lie on the dining table amidst a debris of newspapers, magazines, medications, Post-its, ballpoint pens.

'I come from a family of talkers,' says Ammu. 'Just imagine being married to a man who speaks as if each word costs him sixty rupees.'

'What?' says George, laughing silently, his shoulders and belly shaking.

He goes back to work. He is ninety-four and gathering his resources for a better time. But somewhere in his mind thought flows clearly, if only from habit, and he knows it is a false idea. There is no time. His life is nearing its end, and it hasn't been enough. There is a place for him, and he hasn't claimed it. He's let the quest pass through him like everything else, as another aspect of the makeshift and haphazard. Why else is he at his wife's ancestral home with no idea how long he'll be there or why he should stay?

My cousin comes to visit with her baby daughter. We drive to the train station to meet her. She steps on to the platform with so many bags that Uma forgets to hug her. She puts her hands on her hips.

'Have you left him or what?' she asks.

Chachiamma rarely replies to questions. She rarely speaks, and spends entire days in her nightclothes gazing towards the river. Or on the back porch puffing away at the cigarettes she's found in her father's desk drawer. When she goes out for a smoke, she leaves the baby with one of us.

Uma and Jacob become fond grandparents, spending hours on the floor entertaining the infant. Her teething and sleep habits are discussed at length. Uma washes her and changes her nappies and talks all the while about God and the Devil and the rapture that is coming. She pronounces it rupture. Ammu prescribes and supervises coconut oil head and foot massages. George asks obscure questions.

The arrangement leaves Chachiamma free to wander around the house and the riverfront. She had once been a talker and dancer, a performer at dinner parties, an influencer whose travel stories appeared on high-traffic websites. She married a man who owned a coffee estate somewhere in the hills and they travelled together for a time. But it had all come unglued and nobody knows why. For someone who used to be online all day long, she rarely looks at her phone. She isn't interested in the news. She doesn't care about the state of the house or the world.

Then comes a beach day. (Abortive.)

A week after her arrival, she finally charges her phone and announces that Uma will look after the baby while I drive her to the nearest beach. She packs sunscreen and towels and bottled water. A thirty-minute drive, then we park by a short stretch of sand crowded with every type of ramshackle venture. Ayurvedic massage parlour. Internet café and beer bar. A travel agency that changes money and sells T-shirts and sarongs. Telephone kiosk and tea stall. All jammed together while on either side unused beachfront stretches into the distance. We go into a shack with a mural of Bishop Tutu and Bob Marley sharing a foot-long conical roll-up. A table with a view of the sea. Near us, a man in a wheelchair drinks alone. A couple sits with their heads close together, the man eats and the woman stares at him, her food untouched.

'What,' says the man.

'The reason I wanted to come here. Do you remember?'

'Animal rights judgement?'

'Twenty years ago. Kerala High Court said circus animals shouldn't be kept in tiny cages, shouldn't be tortured by trainers. Said animals deserve dignity like everyone else. How extraordinary is that?'

'It is extraordinary, I grant you.'

The man puts ketchup on his plate, dips his sandwich and takes a good bite.

'Kerala of all places.'

'I agree,' he says, chewing. 'Entirely.'

'And yet there you are with your roast pork sandwich.'

'Yes, Vyoma, because I'm entitled to a little dignity too.'

'Not at the cost of causing agony to an intelligent creature that has done you no harm.'

'I'm sympathetic, I am, but I'd like to lunch in peace.'

She says nothing and watches him chew. He stops, picks up the remains of his sandwich, wraps it in a napkin and leaves the restaurant. Vyoma gazes after him, as if something she has long wondered about has been decided in that instant. Then she too gets up and leaves.

'People spout such nonsense when they think nobody's bloody listening,' says the man in the wheelchair.

I shrug. Chachiamma doesn't look up from her phone.

'My name's Ashok Kush, NRI,' he says. 'You are?'

'Jeet.'

'And you?'

'Chachi, not NRI.'

'On holiday or work?'

'I'm not sure,' I say.

'Lucky man.'

'I've been looking at churches.'

'What's the book you're carrying?'

'A study of Vasco da Gama's letters to the Zamorin of Kerala.'

'Can I make a tiny guess?'

'How tiny?'

'I'll bet that nothing has changed and everything is as hopeless as it ever was.'

'There's always hope, even here,' I say.

'There's always hope, except here. You're thinking, look at this NRI, lives in a nice house in a rich country, visits once a year, and only has contempt for his native land.'

'Funny, that's exactly what I was thinking,' says Chachiamma.

She stands up to take a photo of the beach and in seconds has posted it with a caption: What's up, beaches?

'For someone who can't walk up a flight of stairs or go into an elevator or cross the street without help, nowhere is worse,' continues Ashok Kush. 'How a society treats its handicapped tells you everything. India can be summed up in one word. Heartlessness. I heard what the woman said about circus animals in a different way than you. Even animals are treated with more dignity than the disabled.'

He takes a deep draught of his beer and lights a cigarette and looks at the sea as if trying to understand its purpose.

'When I land in New Delhi, the first thing that occurs to me is, oh, I must adjust my idea of self-worth. I must forget about personal dignity.'

'I feel the same way,' says Chachiamma. 'Not just in New Delhi, in New York and New Iberia as well. Do you have another cigarette?'

She checks her phone. Already her post has two hundred and forty-two likes, eleven shares and numerous comments. When Ashok Kush offers cigarettes, she says she doesn't want one after all.

'I keep trying to quit,' she says dreamily. 'Maybe you never quit, maybe you only take breaks. I don't know.'

'In my opinion? People get the system they deserve. Indians deserve corruption,' says Ashok Kush. 'Imagine what it must be like for me to use a bathroom in India. In my opinion, people get the toilets they deserve also. Perhaps Indians deserve a hole in the ground.' He drops his cigarette to smoulder in the ashtray. 'Forgive me, I'll stop now, I've had too much beer.' But he continues to drink.

'I wish you'd stop,' says Chachiamma. 'If you don't live here, don't criticize.'

A woman comes into the café and nods at us. She takes hold of the handles on his chair and starts to wheel him out.

'Meet my wife and saviour.'

There are hellos all around.

'By the way, Vasco da Gama was buried at the St Francis church. It isn't far, you know. You should go.'

'I was there last week.'

'Did you know he died in Cochin, Christmas Eve, 1524, on his third visit to our glorious country? He's not here any more, of course, they took his remains to Lisbon. Lucky man.' Then, to Chachiamma: 'Apologies.'

The heat has passed its high point and the water is warm from a day of sun. I pick up the beach bag.

'You know what?' she says. 'Let's go home. I'm in no mood. That Ashok Kush? Man, what a downer.'

Uma is right, her church is nothing like the St Francis church. A concrete room with a single window that sheds only a smidgen of light on the unimaginable proceedings within. Ammu notes the lack of floor mats and pews and pictures. No seating, which makes the new pain in her bones impossible to ignore. No furnishings at all except for a tall wooden box in lieu of a pulpit. Oh, and an overpowering smell of disinfectant.

'If the disinfectant smells so bad, I can only imagine what the infectant is like,' says Ammu, holding on to her cane.

George is looking at the congregation, some two dozen in all, not a bad turnout for a home-made church. But it is already steamy and the door to the room is shut. The disinfectant isn't strong enough to counter the tang of all those people packed into a small space. Some sway where they sit or whoop or moan and kneel on the concrete. Some speak Pentecostally in tongues. There is jabbering and false laughter. They turn to Uma with the rapt faces of cultists.

'Takes the cake,' says George. 'Offensive, even to a Christian Hindu like yours sincerely.'

Only the baby seems relaxed as Uma delivers her sermon in a sinister low-pitched voice they've never heard, a diatribe against the Antichrist with the name of a disciple, a young man with a wife and child, and when you look into his flat eyes you see a black pool masked by a robot's face. This man owns your screens, wants to own all of you, hold you close, embrace you, imprison you, wants you to hate. Look at your screen. See the boys and girls living together, coupling and recoupling, encouraged to be here for love, boys and girls who have never left their home towns before, living together on an island, asking how will we find love in real life, much less on TV, and if they do, or pretend to, they're rewarded in dollars. Here she pauses to take a drink of water as shouts of hallelujah break out, followed by a round of piteous crying somewhere close. A group in front bursts into a loose approximation of a Gregorian chant. It is drowned out by fresh cheers.

'Why're they cheering at the mention of money?' says George.

'Don't start,' says Ammu. 'This stupid concrete floor is bad enough.'

Uma asks whose idea it was to make love-hunger equal money-hunger. Who was CEO of brimstone? Who envisioned the melting Himalayas? Remember Noah, she says. Remember the Ark. In the meantime, be like the birds. Migrate. Go east for beginning, west for end. Be like the salmon strayers. The lost ones make the new world.

But even as she speaks the new gospel of Mark, Uma looks at the water bottle in her hand and sees the blazing sword entrusted to her alone, God's sword to guard the gates of paradise. Its fiery tip pointing backwards in time to the sailing ships that brought Thomas the Twin first to north-west India, then to China, then to the shores of Malabar, and even further back to the words spoken by Christ to Thomas, the harsh words that sent him across the ocean, Blessed are they that have not seen and yet have believed, words that stung so deep the young disciple went forth as witness to the ends of the earth. A handful of coins bought him a few feet of space on the deck of a merchant ship, where he pitched a tent, whiling away the hours in the company of the upright and transverse beams at the prow, in the shape of an H with a double crossbar, the Dioscuri, twins and half-brothers Castor and

Pollux, emblems of immortality but also of death, sworn protectors of sailors against shipwreck under doom-laden skies.

Ammu hears strangled shouts. A respectable-looking family of four speaking uninhibitedly in tongues. Perhaps it is the same tongue. Then she remembers a day from long ago, a memory she has suppressed all these years. Her mother in distress, praying in broken Aramaic, begging for her daughter's life. *Barachimo, slomo, barachimo, slomo.*

The chanting starts up again.

'Damnation,' says George happily. 'Not denomination.'

Chachiamma gets up as soon as the sermon is over and picks up the baby. A small hand clutches her finger in fear, or is it joy? What did her daughter understand of these voices raised in plainsong and madness? Whatever it was, it appears to please her. She can't understand it. How sweet-tempered is her child, when she was anything but.

We go out to the car park in the back of the dirt yard in which the church has been raised.

'There's not much I agree with her about, but she's on the money when it comes to marriage,' Chachiamma says.

We turn off the main village road and take the path to the river while she plays a YouTube video on her phone. She and the baby have identical expressions as they watch. I catch some of the lyrics. Gonorrhoea rhymed with Korea. Tokyo with ho. Something about doing Asians.

'Hello?'

'Steel Panther hit, "Asian Hooker",' she says. 'You mean you don't know the band? Other notable numbers include "Poontang Boomerang", "Fat Girl" and "Always Gonna be a Ho".'

'Heavy.'

'My husband's playlist. He loves this song. Sings along every time. *Sucky fucky, sucky fucky, smells like sushi.*'

'Maybe it's a joke band, a parody, like Spinal Tap or Eric Clapton playing reggae?'

'It's no joke. You should see the fans, sea of white dudes in black tees. I told him I prefer K-pop. You know, innocence and primary colours, choreography as sacrament. As far removed from real life as you're likely to get. Hey, look, she likes it.'

In her lap, the baby is dancing.

'We'd been travelling. Spain, Morocco, Vietnam. Then I got pregnant and we came home. It was a huge fight, all because I couldn't stand Steel Panther. He wanted me to shut down my website, said I should stop posting pictures, stop travelling. One morning, he went to work, I came here. I miss him sometimes, so help me God. Then I play his music and I don't miss him at all.'

Ammu gets her wish. A boat to take her on the Muvattupuzha. George refuses even to consider it. He can't swim and it is too late to learn. And there is one more thing.

'Your people don't believe in life preservers,' he says to Ammu.

'My people?'

'River people.'

'We've been preserving very well so far.'

'Without life preservers. Or jackets. Or belts. Or flotation devices of any kind.'

'We don't need them. We can swim.' Not strictly true, she knows. In her newly weakened state, she wouldn't be able to swim very far.

When her father was alive, the boathouse was full of vessels. Narrow canoes the width of a man's foot and wide-bottomed boats that could seat a dozen people. Under the new management, some of the boats wear holes the size of someone's head. Jacob cleans up the only serviceable canoe, points it upstream and pushes off, rowing against the current towards the other side. On both banks, trees sprout into the sky, framing images. A river temple. Women washing vessels and clothes. A makeshift landing stage churned by many feet. Ammu puts her hand into the green water and touches a moment that had occurred, is occurring, would occur in the future.

'The river smells different today,' she says. 'It's going to rain.'

An hour later, in the middle of the day, the sky goes from blue to black. The wind breaks dry branches to the ground. Birds fly helter-skelter. In the small hours of the night, a sudden coolness. Such a relief from the heat that it wakes me with a dream of air conditioning. Then the skies break and rain drops on the roof-tiles with the sound of stones. The storm tears rents in the banana leaves and churns the river into froth. At dawn, I see red pools in the gravel of the courtyard. Beyond, where the paddy fields begin, there is only muddy foam and rain haze. I am at the window when the door creaks open and a frail figure stands in the half-light.

'Boy,' Ammu says, 'do you know it rained like this the day you were born? I almost died because your head was too big. Your grandmother allowed no more births in this house after yours.'

'Really? I had no idea. You never said this before.'

She gives a short laugh and tugs at the scarf she wears like a belt for the pain in her lower back.

'I want to ask you something.'

'Ask anything you want.'

'Do you ever regret it?'

'Regret what?'

'Going through all of that? The childbirth. For me.'

She comes to the window and watches the rain slowly brightening on the fields, hands lifted to her face.

'I'm your mother. I don't regret anything except growing old. I regret that you got old and now I can't hold my little boy's hand.' She sits on the bed, her eyes held by the haze outside. 'I always thought it was a bad bargain. You're born. You're young and you marry. Make your own family. Then everything goes one by one. Your health goes. Everyone you love dies. What kind of bargain is that?'

'We don't have much say in it.'

'But we have to believe. I don't regret anything I did. Maybe I regret some things I didn't do.'

'You're telling me I should do what I want?'

'Yes. Do everything. You want eggs for breakfast?'

'As long as you don't tell me that story about how you almost died, my head was too big, et cetera, et cetera.'

It is still dark after breakfast when my aunt and uncle say they will go across the river to see Esha, their older daughter. She is in a wheelchair, and they worry that the river, which has risen through the night, will flood her house. Ammu and George will go with them. Uma asks me to look after my cousin and the baby.

'The support staff is there to help,' Jacob says, nodding at the old cook, a family retainer who has lived in the house all her life. 'A little hard of hearing, but she's dependable.'

Uma has dressed for the occasion, paisley shawl draped over her Ethiopian dress and headscarf. She sports low-heeled shoes and a big purse. Jacob places a case in the prow of the big canoe. Ammu and George sit stiffly on the wide wooden seat at the back.

In the distance, a soft wash of thunder.

'Don't worry,' says Ammu. 'These big boats are stable.'

George, nervous, grips his wife's hand. Ammu grips her cane.

The old pattern continues, established in the first days of their marriage. When it comes to travel, to finance, to taking charge, it is Ammu who does the work. But in their life of wandering, it is George who is easy with displacement. He makes it a habit to reduce his possessions to a small case for long periods if necessary. As the years pass, it becomes a general practice. Reduce. Divest. Keep only what you need. The older he gets, the shakier his sense of self-worth. He leaves the good brandy on the shelf and prefers cheap army rum. He uses a teaspoon rather than a knife and fork. Ammu treats herself better. But she who has bought and sold houses has tired of setting up new homes. She wants to stay in one place. She is too old for the rigours of Elsewhere.

A light rain starts as they set off for Maneed. It seems to George that the flat-bottomed canoe heaves in the water like a flimsy bath toy. The river has swollen against itself. He believes every story he's heard of the fools who drowned because they underestimated its ferocity. Boats that capsized in an instant. Bloated bodies that floated by, always in the exact middle of the current. Suicides and murders the river had hosted. He believes all of it and understands why it's called the Muvattupuzha, three rivers in one. Because of its size and crushing, intimidating sweep. Now, on top of everything, the rain. Heavy and getting heavier. Ammu unfurls a large black umbrella and positions it over them. She waves as the boatmen row in tandem to the opposite bank.

KURIEN APPEARS THAT AFTERNOON as if he's been watching the house, waiting for Uma and Jacob to leave. I hear men's voices in the courtyard. The older one speaks softly into a cell phone wedged between shoulder and ear. His arms hang loosely simian. The other is a stocky man in a checked lungi who holds an umbrella for his companion. The old cook says something, and both men peer into the windows of the house. I retreat instinctively into the shadows behind the grandfather clock. The doorbell rings. When I open, the man with the cell phone walks past me and inspects the room as if he were evaluating the furniture and the light fixtures. Admittedly, they are in need of repair. On the left side of his face, from eye to ear, a stain the size and shape of a fig, textured like pebble-grained shoe leather.

'I am Jacob's friend,' he says. 'Kurien.'

'Could you leave the umbrella outside?'

'For you,' he says, extending a card, *M.T. Kurien, Accountant,* embossed in blue. 'I want to hold a party here tomorrow night.'

His companion in the doorway has the bulk of a bodyguard or professional wrestler. He stands with his legs impressively apart, lungi damply folded against the oiled slabs of his calves. I wonder how these men have managed to get into the house. Why hadn't I barred the way?

'A party,' I say. 'In this weather?'

'Surely,' says the simian Mr Kurien, staring at the ancient Grundig tube radio, an Anniethottam showpiece. Then his stare comes back to me. 'You are staying alone?'

'I'm looking after the place for my uncle.'

'You are from?'

'Bombay. Mr Kurien, it won't be possible to have a party here.'

'But you can join with us. I've already informed some people.'

He stops. He's said too much. He's invited guests for a party the following night without confirming that the house is available. The stain on his face turns a deeper shade of purple.

'You must not let me down,' he says.

The words are softly spoken but they sound like a threat.

'I'll call my uncle,' I say.

'Yes,' says Kurien, happy now. 'Yes, you call Jacob and ask. Give me his number.'

Chachiamma comes into the room and stops short on seeing the two men. She carries a glossy magazine, and she's wearing a cotton nightdress, the kind of garment Indian housewives favour when they aren't expecting company. She hugs the magazine to her chest and seems about to say something, but turns and leaves the room.

Kurien says, 'Your wife?'

'My uncle's daughter.'

'You can both join with us for the party.'

'She's not well,' I say. 'She's here to rest.'

The cook is on the phone with Babu, a family friend I've been told to call if I need help while my uncle and aunt are away. She holds the receiver in Kurien's direction.

'For you, saar.'

'Hello, hello. I'm Kurien, friend of Jacob. I want the house tomorrow evening, no need for kitchen, only rooms.' He listens for a moment. Then: 'Yes, yes. For party. Party!'

He hangs up and says, 'The girl, she will join us?'

I lead him to the porch, and we stand under the dripping eaves.

I say, 'I have your card. I'll call you.'

He looks at the water run-off at the corner of the house.

'My son is also in Bombay,' he says, and waits.

He leaves reluctantly, under the umbrella held by his companion. The landline rings two hours later. I am on the back porch wondering when the rain will stop. I remember Uma's sermon and imagine an unsinkable torpedo-equipped ark.

'Did you speak to Jacob? It's Kurien.'

He rings an hour later and at intervals through the evening. Around midnight, the phone rings again. I let it ring for some time. When I pick up, there is only silence. I listen to his troubled breathing. He doesn't speak and he doesn't hang up.

Late at night, I patrol the perimeter with the machete Jacob uses to cut coconuts. I sleep in the easy chair in the front room. I wake early and patrol. I take my duties seriously. On my rounds, I find a cloudy shaving mirror hooked to a beam on the back porch. I notice I've grown a beard. You look into a mirror at your own peril. You don't know what lies behind that bland façade. Doppelganger. Future ghost. Evil twin. Look at that man, you think. How many wrong turns did it take to bring him to the house of his birth with no reason to stay or to go?

'After all I'm my father's son,' I tell the bearded face.

It rains for three days and Bible-black nights. Sound-maddened hours. The river overflows its banks and the paddies flood. Water climbs the coconut trees in the backyard and surrounds the house. I hear stranded cows and dogs on the short hills around us.

Chachiamma gives me a list of items for the house. I unhook a canoe and row across the paddy fields to the main road. At the shop, I pick up soap, coconut oil, sanitary napkins, milk sachets, instant coffee, instant noodles, cigarettes, and put them in a plastic bag and hook the bag to my belt. The bottom of the boat is puddled with mud and rainwater.

She is waiting on the front porch and rushes to me before I step off the boat. Handing me the baby, she rummages in the bags. The baby regards me calmly as her mother lights a Gold Flake and paces the length of the porch. Chachiamma crosses her arms and holds two fingers in front of her and blows the smoke away from us.

'I can feel it,' she says. 'Very soon something will happen. Can't you feel it too?'

THE FLOOD SPARES ESHA'S HOUSE, but not the grounds. Jacob, Uma and the cook stack what fruit can be saved in the kitchen. Jackfruit and mangoes and lemons, to be preserved and pickled. But much fruit is lost, smashed to the ground by heavy winds. Some younger trees, guavas, figs and custard apple, are uprooted or drowned. When the floods recede, Jacob looks for labourers to clear the mess. Two men arrive. Migrants from the north, wiry, muscular, shifty-eyed. They speak little Malayalam. Even so, they manage to indicate how uninterested they are in the work. Any task Jacob hasn't mentioned at the outset they refuse to do. Quarrels occur. In a few hours, matters deteriorate so much that Jacob threatens to flog the men with a switch he pulls from a neem tree. They wait until after lunch and throw down their tools and leave, swearing in Bihari or Bhojpuri or whatever alien tongue they've been speaking all day.

The nationalism Ammu had experienced in Bombay fifty-five years earlier has taken root even in Kerala, even within her youngest, most carefree brother. He takes to making scathing comments about North Indians, particularly Biharis, who make up most of the migrant labour in Kerala.

'We should secede from the Indian Union,' he says.

'I've been saying this for years,' says George.

'The Republic of Kerala,' says Jacob. 'What have northerners given us other than their choicest insults? They impose their language on us, denigrate us. Treat us like another race.'

'Quite right,' says George.

'Why should we not do the same?'

'We should.'

'We should tie their hands behind their backs and beat that ugly language out of their heads. With chappals!'

George understands that Jacob is serious about secession in a way he has never been. But Jacob is convinced he's found a sympathizer in his brother-in-law. Malayalam-language pamphlets begin to appear around the Maneed house. Ominous titles. *Out!* and *Why Are They Here?* These, Jacob will leave in George's room and George will return unread.

It is the toddy shop incident that makes Ammu decide they have to go home to Bangalore. There she will feel less of an outsider than in the village in which she's been raised.

Jacob is at the tea shop on the main road of Maneed, a village smaller than Mamalassery. A few roadside stores, a bus stop, a granary. At the tea shop, he eats a plate of banana fritters and drinks a glass of strong milk tea and waits for people he knows. On a chit of paper, with a pencil stub he makes calculations. How much he has paid the labourers, what work they have completed, how much remains to be done.

'Looking for workers to clean the yard, daughter's house, you know, but only outsiders available,' he says. 'What they're like, don't ask.'

He speaks as if joking, and so his jokes are met with jokes.

'Don't we all know,' says the district MLA, his lungi folded at the knees, a thin towel around his head.

'Robbery,' says Jacob, rounding off the sums on his chit. 'Straight-face robbery.'

'We'll be climbing our own trees, tapping our own toddy.'

'If they're not interested in honest money for honest work, why come here from Bihar and Uttar Pradesh?'

The legislator blows on his tea and takes no sides. His job is to smooth over quarrels not fan them, a trait that feeds his popularity.

Unhappy with the response to his troubles, Jacob goes to the door and watches the rain grow heavier. Its hiss drowns the voices and clatter of the shop. The sky is getting dark. The tea shop's lights come on: two naked bulbs on grease-encrusted wires. A bus goes past and stops. A group of schoolchildren get off and unfurl their umbrellas, splashing their gumboots into the deepest roadside puddles.

'Saw you go into the toddy shop first thing this morning,' says the tea shop owner, who owes Jacob a little over two thousand rupees for an order of rubber matting.

'Rain,' says Jacob. 'When it rains, I want toddy.'

'It's the wet season. You'll be wanting toddy all the time.'

'Put the chai on my tab, we'll square it later?'

Jacob hurries across the road into a side street and enters the toddy shop. Only one of the thatched cubicles that lines the front yard is free. He asks the boy to light an oil lamp and takes a seat at the grimy plastic table and orders toddy and fish fry. The toddy, brought in a fly-specked bottle, has fermented during the day. It tastes better than it had when he'd drunk it fresh first thing in the morning. Each sip goes a long way in making him feel better. He hears voices from the adjoining cubicle separated by a rotting thatch wall. Two men he knows, Thampan and Pulayan, men who had worked on his farm some years earlier but are now well-off enough to hire their own labourers to work on their own farms. How has the world changed so quickly?

'Boys,' he says, putting his head above the partition. 'I'm looking for workers, you know.'

'So, it's true,' says Thampan. 'I heard, I heard. Believe me, if I knew of a fellow, I'd hire him myself.'

He tells a story concerning a man Jacob remembers from his sister Ammu's wedding:

'You know Pathrose? Came back from the Gulf with bags of Arab money to build a new house? The house his grandfather built wasn't grand enough for the Gulf returnee? Bought a plot near the river, but he couldn't get anyone to carry the stones for the gate or move the sand to lay the foundations. The labourers who'd been doing the work all these years started yelling about workers' rights. Union this, union that. Nobody wanted to work.

'So Pathrose got a plan. He went to Cochin and found labourers. Three men happy to do anything. Drove them to Mamalassery in his own car. Put on his work clothes, one torn shirt and old lungi, helped them do the work. They started to unload, and a gang of toughs came. "Bloody bastard," said the boss, big fellow with a Veerappan bandit moustache, "who told you to work in our area?" The three men he'd brought from Cochin ran for their lives. What did old man Pathrose do? He paid the union gangsters and removed the sand with his own hands. They sat and watched.'

The two men laugh uproariously, their hilarity fuelled by fermented toddy, but Jacob cannot join in.

Then he hears the language from that morning, Bihari or Bhojpuri or Haryanvi or whatever tongue the northerners had been speaking. They are drinking in the next cubicle. He hears his name and he hears a laugh. Are they laughing at him? He goes into the cubicle and notes their size, the size of their fists, the muscular arms and stubby scarred hands. A slap ensues. He isn't sure how. He didn't plan to do it, but it seems he's slapped the taller one. Without planning to do so, he does it again. The man leans his head against the thatch wall and begins to sob. His friend rises to his feet, face blotchy from drink and rage.

'Ghar,' he keeps saying in Hindi. 'Tera ghar.'

Only later does Jacob understand that the man was saying he knew the location of Jacob's house and that he and his family weren't safe. Which is when he wishes he'd slapped them both a few times, slapped the idea right out of their heads.

The owner of the toddy shop tells the men no fighting is allowed on the premises and it would be better if they left. His words are meant for Jacob, but he addresses them to the newcomers. He too owes Jacob money for teakwood purchased for his home. The two men finish their drink, insisting all the while they are owed money for the morning's work. They take their time gathering their things, the taller one dry-eyed at last, thank God, and Jacob feeling guilty now, handing over hundred-rupee notes and telling the men to hop on the first bus north. The way he says the word north gives it the inflection of a curse.

When the labourers, who aren't labourers but fishermen, leave the toddy shop, fortified by a bottle each of the fermented variety, they climb on the moped they've rented and ride slowly back to their guest house, chatting about their economic prospects in the back of beyond that is Mamalassery and whether or not it is time to move Elsewhere, and how much mightier is the Siang compared to the Muvattupuzha, in which it is difficult if not impossible to fish. They are speaking Assamese, not Bihari or Bhojpuri or Haryanvi, and they are not from Uttar Pradesh but migrants from Kashmir whose families had settled first in the Punjab and then near the Siang River in Arunachal Pradesh. The bigger one, who'd been reduced to tears by Jacob's slap, tries to ignore the attractions of the landscape they are riding through, the lush green so different from the regions through which they'd travelled to reach the south, a journey of four days by train. They'd gone all the way to Kanyakumari, the southernmost tip of the country, with the idea of returning in stages to Punjab and finding work wherever work was to be found. His smaller, wilier companion, who is steering the rickety two-wheeler along the potholed mud roads, suggests a move to Cochin where the fishing industry is always looking for men to work the Chinese nets, or so he's heard. The rain gets heavier, which makes the road harder to negotiate. The potholes, filled with yellow mud and rainwater, blur into burnt ochre and become more dangerous. It is difficult to tell how deep the holes are, the only advantage being that it makes driving dangerous for all vehicles, and if they were to come across a car or scooter stuck in a ditch, they could offer their services for a reasonable consideration. They are approaching the junction near the bus stop for Piravom and debating the poor agricultural prospects of the region as compared to their home village, when the smaller man manoeuvring the moped sees a shadowy, possibly female figure moving swiftly across the road, moving sideways, dancing nimbly across the puddles as if she were walking on water, a large woman with matted hair under a conical witch's hat that is dry despite the heavy rain. Slowing the moped to a crawl, he asks his friend if he's seen anything, a witch for example. 'Don't stop,' says the man riding pillion, 'there's no one there.' 'I'm telling you, I saw a witch,' says his partner, slowing almost to a stop, his eyes never leaving the spot at the side of the road where the figure had disappeared. 'She's wearing a robe made of upside-down golden crosses and a hood or a hat.' 'Ride,' says his partner fearfully, 'ride fast, let's get out of this place.' Like all fishermen, they are firmly superstitious, and by now both men are sure they are being hunted by evil spirits from the unfathomable south. The moped puts on a sudden burst of speed and its front wheel immediately goes into a pothole throwing both men to the road. 'Damn, damn and fuck,' says the smaller fisherman. 'Can't you watch where you're going?' says the bigger man. 'You almost...' He doesn't finish, for at that moment he too sees the witch, a woman covered in crosses, under a pointed hat of some sort. He jumps up and runs towards the main road, vaulting across the puddles in his way. His friend leaves the moped where it lies and takes off after him. They disappear into the night and the pouring rain.

When Jacob gets home and tells the story about how he had run into the labourers from Uttar Pradesh or Bihar, Ammu is properly appalled. Even Esha seems troubled. The sweet smile she usually wears vanishes in an instant, to be replaced by a look of anxiety. Only Uma and George think of the fracas as ordinary, something to be expected from Jacob.

'Such drama,' says George.

'Unnecessary drama,' says Uma, who's just come home from her evening walk, for which she always wears her Ethiopian habesha kemiz festooned with gold crosses of all sizes, a perfectly loose and comfortable shirt for the brisk bit of exercise she takes, come rain or shine. She takes off the pointed old umbrella hat of palm leaves that she's waterproofed with coconut oil, leaves it against the wall of the porch, and goes in to change her wet walking clothes.

'I'm going home,' Ammu tells Jacob. 'With or without you.'

Without, as it turns out.

Jacob and Uma stay with Esha: it is still raining.

I'M TRYING TO RAISE AN ENGLISH STATION on the Grundig, dialling past swatches of static, lighting briefly on old Hindi film songs, those plaintive rain-flecked melodies that seem always to be floating on India's airwaves. '*Kabhi kabhi mere dil mein*' and '*Baharon phool barsao*' and '*Chura liya hai tumne jo dil ko*', when I hear Chachiamma calling from the back porch.

'I'm sure I saw it,' she says. 'A boat.'

Brownish water streaked with river run-off and paddy mud has reached the top steps. I look towards the river and see nothing but haze. The tallest palms have melted into it. By a trick of the eye, shapes form in the mist, form and break up. One resolves into the prow of a canoe. Then comes the flat thwack of heavy wood striking the steps. The boatman jumps out and holds the vessel steady for Ammu and George.

It isn't much of a welcome. Chachiamma takes Ammu's case, I take George's. There is tea. Beds are made. The cook prepares a meal. We light the lamps (the electricity has failed again) and fill them in on what has happened. When she hears about Kurien, Ammu says:

'Keep the machete handy. Two UP bhaiyas may also pay us a visit.'

But nobody comes. Not Kurien and not the bhaiyas. The rain grows into a downpour and doesn't stop for a week. The water climbs across the porch and into the living room. We move the carpets out of the way, but some of the furniture can't be saved. The teak dining table. The big bed I'd been born in. The double-jointed easy chairs. All are submerged, all ruined. Some cots, books, photo albums and medicines, the old Grundig, a small fridge, foodstuffs and plates, these things we carry up to the attic. We spread carpets on the floor. Ammu and George entertain the baby while Chachiamma watches the rain through the arched windows. The cook manages to use the wood stove in the kitchen though she has to wade through knee-deep water and watch for river snakes. George works on his manuscript. I search the photo albums. It is almost like a normal day in the life.

Ammu flips the pages of an album and stops at a faded black-and-white photo, one of its corners missing. 'That's your father the day he came out of jail. He knew when he stepped out of Hazaribagh there would be press from all over the world. He put on a suit, even in that heat. He's better dressed than I am. All I could think was, my God, why do they call this place Hazaribagh, where are the thousand gardens, I don't see a single one. I was thinking we had to leave Bihar. After all the publicity, the chief minister will want revenge. In a week, we were back in Bombay.'

'What's this?'

'The first letter your father wrote to me. From America. I saved it just in case. He didn't save any of mine.'

'At least one of you thought ahead.'

'Take the pictures, in case you write about this one day.'

'The way things are going?' says George. 'Do it soon. Between the rain and the melting ice caps, we'll be under water sooner than you think.'

And the rain keeps falling, pitilessly, on the drowned and soon-to-be-drowned, met with thunder and forked lightning and the lowing of cows. When it lets up, we have become used to living with water. We know how to dress for it. We've adjusted so well that when the flood recedes and the sodden floors and forgotten knick-knacks show themselves, in a stench of damp and rot, we have to acclimatize again to dryness. To land that does not shift under our feet. Then the sun returns, bright and hot, which makes the stench unbearable.

Ammu begins to pack the day Jacob and Uma return. Arrangements are made for a car to Cochin and a flight out. In the evening, there are the old sounds. The grinding of spices, voices from the porch and kitchen, the noise of repairs around the house. Chachiamma goes to the inner room where Uma and the baby are already asleep. Jacob returns late and lies reading on the couch in the front room. George turns his face away from the light and is soon asleep. Ammu stands at the porch for a long time and listens to the sounds of the place she has thought of as home for most of her life. It is no longer so.

Now it seems to Ammu she has no home, for home is no longer a city or a country and the people in them, but the rooms of the houses in which she's lived. The big bedroom she shared with her sisters at Anniethottam. The teacher's quarters, two cots to a room, in Alwaye. The small front room in Mahim that served as both living and dining room, the city outside, just steps away from the floor she shared with her new husband. The balcony that ran the length of the apartment by the Arabian Sea on Cadell Road. The front room of the apartment at Pataliputra Housing Colony that became a meeting place for students. She'd taken care of the children there while George was in jail. The small living room of the apartment in Shirin Building, near Navy Nagar in Colaba. The bedroom of their first apartment in Hong Kong, at Arts Mansion. The kitchen of the second on McDonnell Road, where she thought of tearing into a hundred pieces the picture of the Vietnamese woman. The view from the apartment in New York, twelve floors up, of the canyons of Seventy-Ninth and York. Sirens at any hour of the night. The large front room of the first apartment she bought in Bombay. A six-inch view of the sea. Palm trees outside the fourth-floor window. The sunken living room of the first house they owned in Bangalore. The sunlit bedroom and garden of the second. The jackfruit tree and the butter fruit.

The remembered rooms unfold in her mind like pictures from an album with sheets of tissue between the pages. They bring vivid sensations that leave her grateful and surprised. She traces herself through the rooms of her life, opening seamlessly one into another, forward and back. So, on a rainy day in Mamalassery, when she steps indoors from the porch, it is to the cold muted light of a northern country. It seems correct then that these memories have lost their sting and can no longer cause hurt or happiness. They are only receptacles to return to her the past.

END AND RETURN

Bangalore, 2025 | Mamalassery, 2025

And on turning the last page, we found the first.

ROOM 403, MANIPAL HOSPITAL. December 2024. The last Sunday before Christmas. Her ragged breathing, the drip of saline, the antibiotic dripping into a separate tube in her neck. Her voice a hoarse whisper. Sometimes, she's so frustrated by her inability to communicate that she gets angry with herself and her son. Then she tries again. She never gives up. She speaks only in Malayalam now, the language in which she's spoken to him all his life. Maybe this is why, so he'd understand her at the end, when she's too tired or in too much of a hurry to speak in English. 'When will I be able to walk again?' she asks. 'Soon,' he says, after a small hesitation. Then, some hours later: 'It isn't cancer or something, is it?' He replies without hesitation this time, as she has trained him. As he's done many times before, he tells her the lie that comforts. Are you on drugs? Of course not. Are you drinking too much? Of course not. Will you be late? Of course not. It isn't cancer or something, is it? Of course not. They have never used the words *cancer* or *multiple myeloma*, though she must suspect it from the trips to the oncology ward, the mention of chemo by a doctor who talks about her in her presence as if she's already gone. 'Well, Christmas is cancelled this year,' she whispers, and silently laughs. 'No,' he says, 'not cancelled, it's postponed. You'll get better soon.' There are balloons in the hallway. The nurses have made a nativity out of discards and old tinsel. They're singing 'Silent Night'. The song in his head has nothing to do with Christmas.

I've been a bad son most of my life. I'm trying to make up for it.

As it turns out, New Year is cancelled too. Early in January, he flies to Kerala, his mother's ashes in a box in his suitcase. He discovers that airline rules disallow ashes in hand baggage. The crematorium attendants have placed her in a clay pot, a sticker on the side with her name and date of cremation, the year wrong:

Ammu George
04/01/24

And this is how they fly, mother and son, south to Cochin, then a rented car into the country for an hour and a half, the unfamiliar new road extending all the way to the house, Anniethottam, where he takes a boat out into the middle of the river, the boatman stroking the water to keep the unsteady fibreglass vessel in place, the current swift and the water clear, time like the current, moving forward and back, to weeks earlier, frail shapes that lift and change, witness to wild fires, wild floods, wild blood that surrounds the mother's hollowed-out bones while her son waits for the drip from a pouch sourced a moment ago, from a blood bank across town, too late now for the blood to replenish her dying platelets, he knows, but anxious he watches the irregular drip and calls a nurse if it slows or stops, the hours passing like days at the equator, slow, clockless, minutes like molasses, and when evening falls and he kisses her face and strokes her hand and says, 'Bye Mama,' he does not know that she will take it as a signal, as permission, and that he will be summoned back to the room within the hour, his sister on the phone saying, 'Hurry, she's going,' though in truth, by the time he returns she has already gone, towards the fire, the electric glow, ashen light he will carry to the house where she, and he, were born, twenty-five years apart, to immerse her in the river that begins this story, the river that becomes sea that becomes ocean, and for all the years of his life when he sees water, he will think, she's here.

INDEX OF PHOTOGRAPHS AND DOCUMENTS

16. *Sister Beatrice, and Ardiane & Barbe Bleue,* Maurice Maeterlinck, Allen & Unwin (1924)
17. Malayalam translation of Baudelaire's 'Epilogue' by A.T. Markose (undated)
18. House with bird, Rue de la Huchette (1988; photograph by the author)
19. Keepsake, Hotel Janpath, New Delhi, courtesy Carol Dey archive (undated)
20. Coffin, Bangalore (2020; photograph by the author)
21. Anniethottam House, Mamalassery (undated, photographer unknown)
22. Boat on the Muvattupuzha (2025, photograph by the author)

ACKNOWLEDGEMENTS

'Woman on a Motorcycle', narrated by John Malkovich, originally appeared in *Alexander*.

'Pourquoi avec son Père?' originally appeared in *Granta*.

'How to Leave a Husband' originally appeared in *Imaginable Worlds: Art, Crisis, and Global Futures* (University of Chicago Press).

ABOUT THE AUTHOR

Jeet Thayil is a poet, novelist and musician. He was born near the Muvattupuzha river in Kerala, and has made his home in various far-flung cities of the world.

HarperCollins *Publishers* India

At HarperCollins India, we believe in telling the best stories and finding the widest readership for our books in every format possible. We started publishing in 1992; a great deal has changed since then, but what has remained constant is the passion with which our authors write their books, the love with which readers receive them, and the sheer joy and excitement that we as publishers feel in being a part of the publishing process.

Over the years, we've had the pleasure of publishing some of the finest writing from the subcontinent and around the world, including several award-winning titles and some of the biggest bestsellers in India's publishing history. But nothing has meant more to us than the fact that millions of people have read the books we published, and that somewhere, a book of ours might have made a difference.

As we look to the future, we go back to that one word—a word which has been a driving force for us all these years.

Read.

Harper Collins · 4th · HARPER FICTION · HARPER NON-FICTION · HARPER BUSINESS · HCCB HARPERCOLLINS CHILDREN'S BOOKS

HARPER DESIGN · Harper Sport · HARPER PERENNIAL · HARPER VANTAGE · हार्पर हिन्दी · BOOKTOPUS